Habits of

SUCCESS

&

WEALTH BUILDING

Unleashing the Power of
Consistency and Growth

Table of contents

Introduction

Many people have the ambition of being successful and accumulating riches, despite the fact that we live in a world that is becoming more competitive. On the other hand, it often appears as if only a select few people are able to achieve the levels of success and financial stability that they have set for themselves. Understanding the routines and mentalities that set apart these successful people from the rest of the population is essential if one wants to realize this potential's full breadth and depth. This book seeks to give a thorough guide to the concepts and practices that may assist in paving the road to personal and financial success, and its goal is to do so in an effort to fulfill that goal.

The adoption of certain habits that are typical of those who are successful and rich is one of the most significant aspects that lead to success and wealth. These habits are also indicative of those who are successful and wealthy. Discipline, perseverance, and a robust work ethic are often involved when it comes to these patterns of behavior. You will be better prepared to begin on the road toward sustainable transformation and accomplishment if you learn and incorporate these routines into your own life.

However, escaping the mindset that you have to work from 9 to 5 is just as important. Our capacity to create, dream on a grand scale, and take the required risks to attain our objectives is often constrained by the old paradigm of the workplace. Those who are prepared to question the status quo may unlock a world of opportunities by first acknowledging the limitations of this thinking and then investigating alternate ways of approaching problems.

It is crucial that you realize that success is built on a foundation of tiny, incremental improvements that generate major benefits over time as you begin on your road. Your is something that you must keep in mind at all times. You may progressively modify your thinking and behaviors by concentrating on these changes and adopting them into your everyday life. This will provide a firm foundation for further development in the future.

The next critical stage is to develop an attitude that is conducive to success. Developing a constructive and proactive outlook on life, outlining your objectives, and retaining a firm faith in your capacity to accomplish those objectives are all necessary steps in this process. A mentality for success involves not just thinking positively but also acting consistently and learning from one's mistakes in order to keep moving ahead. Thinking positively is simply one component of this attitude.

It is impossible to understate the importance of being consistent. It is the engine that propels the formation of new routines, the realization of objectives, and the upkeep of success over the long run. You may develop a momentum that will carry you toward your goals if you cultivate consistency in your activities and choices. This will help you get closer to achieving those objectives.

Building successful relationships and networks is an additional critical component of achieving success and amassing money. Building a solid network of contacts and forming connections with people who share your interests and values may help you get access to a variety of opportunities and resources that would not be available to you otherwise. Your chances of being successful in both your personal and professional lives may be significantly increased by putting effort into cultivating these connections and investing in your network of contacts.

One of the most important keys to achieving success and developing money is to make investments in both yourself and your future. This involves a wide variety of actions, including maintaining a healthy lifestyle, developing new skills, searching out educational opportunities, and creating a solid support system. You are establishing the basis for a rich and rewarding future by making the development of yourself and your personal relationships a top priority.

Strategies for accumulating wealth are essential components for reaching both financial stability and freedom. By gaining an understanding of the fundamentals of saving, investing, and producing numerous sources of income, you may help yourself amass money over the course of time, which will provide you the flexibility to follow your goals and aspirations without being constrained by financial considerations.

The road toward enduring transformation is an individual one that is personal and one of a kind for each person. You may start to alter your life and construct a path toward success and prosperity that is suited to your individual needs and desires if you embrace the ideas and techniques that are presented in this book and put them into practice in your daily activities. You will be well-equipped to overcome difficulties and build a future that is defined by your own vision of success if you are determined, consistent, and have a growth mindset. The path may be tough, but if you do so, you will be able to create a future that is defined by your own vision of success.

Chapter 1

The Habits of the Successful and Wealthy

People who want to be prosperous and successful typically pay careful attention to the behaviors of individuals who are already there and try to model their own behaviour after those behaviors. Even if there is no one-size-fits-all recipe for success, there are some behaviors that seem to regularly contribute to the successes of people who are both financially successful and professionally accomplished.

The development of a strong work ethic is one of the most important practices that successful people make a point to cultivate. This requires not just putting in long hours but also using your head while you're doing it. People that are successful tend to prioritize their work and put their attention on the things that are the most essential and meaningful to them rather than just attempting to get as much done as they can. They are also aware of the significance of delegating tasks to others and using the skills of those around them in order to make the most of their own time and resources.

One such practice that is typical of prosperous people is a dedication to continuing their education throughout their lives. They are aware that in order to maintain a competitive advantage in a world that is always evolving, they need to continuously educate themselves and develop new abilities. This may entail engaging in activities such as reading books, going to seminars, or taking classes in subjects related to their areas of interest or competence. They are better equipped to negotiate changes and take advantage of new possibilities if they continue to educate themselves and remain flexible.

It is impossible to overstate the importance of building relationships for those who aim to be prosperous and successful. There are a great number of successful people who also have an extensive contact list that they have built up over the course of their lives. They are aware of the significance of cultivating strong connections and keeping relationships, as they recognize that doing so may result in the development of new possibilities, partnerships, and collaborations. They build a network of folks who are more likely to provide support to them when it is required by demonstrating a genuine interest in the well-being of others and by providing assistance whenever it is feasible.

One of the most important traits of successful individuals is their capacity to define their objectives in crystal-clear terms. They are able to plot a route toward their desired results if they first articulate what it is that they want to accomplish and then divide that goal into a series of stages that are more attainable. In addition, they make it a habit to evaluate and modify their objectives on a regular basis to ensure that they are proceeding in the right direction and making significant headway.

Another essential habit that separates those who are successful and affluent from others is the ability to manage their time effectively. They are aware that time is a limited resource. Therefore they make sure to distribute it in the most effective manner possible. This often entails assigning priorities to various activities and making use of various tools and methods in order to increase productivity. They are also aware of the significance of establishing boundaries in order to have a good work-life balance, which may aid in the prevention of burnout and protect their general health and well-being.

People that are successful also often have the ability to have a good attitude and exhibit perseverance in the face of adversity. They are often able to reframe failures as chances for growth and continue to keep their attention on their goals, even when they are confronted with challenges. They are able to maintain their adaptability and openness to change because they have developed a growth mentality, which enables them to persist and, in the end, accomplish their objectives.

Another characteristic that is shared by successful people and affluent people is financial discipline. They often maintain a lifestyle that is commensurate with their financial resources and make a concerted effort to both save money and intelligently invest it. This requires them to have a sound financial strategy, establish budgets, and make well-informed judgments on their assets. They have been able to amass and maintain their riches over the course of time thanks to the prudent management of their finances.

Key habits that successful and wealthy people share

Habits that are formed and maintained over a period of time may often be traced back to the origins of success and prosperity. We may get a deeper understanding of the guiding principles behind successful people's accomplishments and learn how to adopt those ideas into our own lives by analysing the important behaviors that are shared by affluent and successful individuals. This digs into a number of behaviors that are often found among affluent people, goes into the meaning of such behaviors, and offers thoughts on how to nurture those behaviors.

Cultivating a Strong Work Ethic

People that are successful often have a strong work ethic, which may be defined as the capacity to work effectively, as well as devotion and perseverance. To cultivate a strong work ethic, one must not only put in long hours but also think critically about how they spend their time at work. This necessitates assigning a priority to each activity according to its significance and worth, delegating duties, and drawing on the expertise of others in order to make the most efficient use of time and resources.

Commitment to Lifelong Learning

Those who are successful and rich are aware of the significance of lifelong education in maintaining their relevance and successfully adjusting to a world that is always evolving. They are better able to grab new chances and handle problems if they are devoted to expanding their knowledge and abilities and continually learning new things. This section will explore a variety of methods, such as reading, attending seminars, and taking courses in subjects of interest or competence, that may be used to develop a habit of learning that continues throughout one's life.

The Power of Networking

Those who want to be prosperous and successful should make it a point to cultivate and keep in touch with a wide circle of influential connections at all times. We will discuss the significance of establishing meaningful connections and cultivating relationships, both of which have the potential to result in the formation of new possibilities, partnerships, and collaborations. In addition to this, we will go through techniques for successful networking and methods for establishing relationships that are mutually useful and supportive of one another.

Goal-Setting and Planning

It is vital to have objectives that are both clear and explicit in order to plot a course that will lead to success and prosperity. Successful people are good at defining goals for themselves, breaking those goals down into stages that are more attainable, and periodically assessing and changing their plans to ensure that they are moving in the right direction. This part of the guide will go into the process of goal-setting and planning, and it will give advice on how to express objectives, establish concrete tasks, and keep on track toward reaching desired results.

Time Management and Productivity

Successful individuals have a critical habit that sets them apart, and that is effective time management. They are aware of the worth of their time and are skilled at managing it in such a way as to achieve optimal levels of productivity. In this part, we will review strategies and applications for improved time management. Some of the topics that will be covered include prioritizing tasks, creating boundaries, and developing routines that promote a good work-life balance.

Maintaining a Positive Attitude and Demonstrating Resilience

People who are successful are characterized by having a good attitude and being resilient. They are often able to reframe failures as chances for growth and continue to keep their attention fixed on their objectives, even in the face of challenges. The necessity of creating a growth mindset, tactics for maintaining optimism even in the face of adversity, and methods for building resilience in order to endure and achieve success are all topics that will be covered in this part.

Financial Discipline and Planning

Maintaining a level of wealth over time requires a disciplined approach to one's own finances. This implies not spending more than one earns, saving and investing money intelligently, and making choices about one's finances after gathering as much information as possible. In this part of the lesson, we will discuss the fundamentals of practicing good financial discipline, such as developing a financial plan, establishing budgets, and selecting investments that are prudent.

Prioritizing Personal Health and Well-being

There are a lot of successful individuals who understand how important it is to keep their physical and mental health in good shape in order to keep their successes going. This part will analyze the relationship between one's personal well-being and achievement, and it will give advice for integrating into one's routine regular exercise, a balanced diet, as well as appropriate rest and relaxation.

Case studies and examples to illustrate the habits

Case Study 1: Elon Musk

Elon Musk, CEO of Tesla and SpaceX, is a shining example of someone who embodies the characteristics of affluent and successful people because of the habits he has developed. Because of his tenacious work ethic, unwavering dedication to continuous education, and uncanny capacity to establish challenging objectives for himself, he has emerged as one of the most successful and important businesspeople of our day.

Musk is renowned for his work ethic, putting in anything from 80 to 100 hours each week on average. He is able to successfully oversee numerous profitable firms at the same time because of his ability to multitask and his unwavering concentration on the work at hand. His commitment to his endeavors exemplifies the significance of working diligently as well as strategically in order to accomplish one's objectives.

Musk's dedication to studying throughout his life is one of the most remarkable elements of his professional life. In spite of the fact that he has degrees in physics and economics, the majority of his knowledge in the domains of rocket science and electric vehicle technology was acquired via independent study. He has frequently attributed his achievement to the fact that he has a strong passion for reading as well as a natural curiosity. As a result of his dedication to lifelong education, he has been able to change a variety of different businesses and develop original approaches to solving difficult challenges.

One further remarkable characteristic of Musk's success is his capacity to formulate daring objectives and aggressively work toward achieving them. His goal for SpaceX, for instance, is to populate Mars and make it possible for life to exist on several planets. Musk has continuously shown progress towards this aim, launching a number of successful missions and producing ground-breaking technology. Some people may see this as an unachievable ambition, yet, Musk has made progress toward this goal. This underlines the significance of creating objectives that are both clear and detailed, as well as keeping consistent in one's pursuit of those goals.

Case Study 2: Oprah Winfrey

In order to triumph over challenges and establish herself as one of the most powerful persons in the media, Oprah Winfrey is a shining example of someone who has developed the behaviors associated with prosperous and successful people. Her path from a difficult childhood to becoming a millionaire is an uplifting example of the power of perseverance, networking, and maintaining a good mindset.

The narrative of Winfrey is one of perseverance and unwavering commitment. She has always found the courage to keep going ahead in spite of the many challenges and disappointments that she has encountered throughout her life, including adversity stemming from poverty and mistreatment. Her persistent confidence in both her own abilities and her capacity to triumph over challenges has been a primary factor in her level of achievement.

The importance of networking in Winfrey's professional life cannot be overstated. Her capacity to form meaningful connections with individuals from a wide variety of backgrounds has enabled her to achieve the level of success that she has achieved. Her genuine interest in other people and her readiness to provide assistance and support has made her a well-liked public figure, and her broad network of contacts has made it possible for her and those around her to take advantage of innumerable new possibilities.

Another important component in Winfrey's success is the optimistic outlook she has maintained throughout her career. She has always approached life with an optimistic and grateful attitude, which has enabled her to stay focused on the objectives she has set for herself and triumph over difficulties. This way of thinking has not only helped her achieve success in her professional life but has also made her a source of motivation for tens of millions of people all over the globe.

Case Study 3: Warren Buffett

The illustrious investor and current CEO of Berkshire Hathaway, Warren Buffett, is yet another example of a person who has mastered the practices that affluent and successful people use. One of the most successful investors in the history of the world as a result of his ability to clearly define objectives, his devotion to learning throughout his life, and his financial discipline.

Buffett's ability to maintain his financial discipline is a significant factor in his overall success. He is well-known for his value-oriented investing strategy, which centers on making long-term investments in cheap firms and purchasing and holding such companies for a period of time. Together with his thriftiness and careful management of resources, this tactic, together with his careful distribution of those resources, has enabled him to acquire a fortune that places him among the wealthiest persons in the world.

Learning throughout one's life is another crucial component in Buffett's formula for achieving success. He has often said that a significant portion of his financial expertise may be ascribed to his voracious reading habits, which have enabled him to acquire a profound grasp of a variety of market movements and businesses. Because of his dedication to lifelong learning, he is able to make well-informed judgments and seize chances that other people would miss.

In addition to this, Buffett is well-known for his ability to establish distinct objectives and have a long-term view. Instead of looking for ways to get quick money, he has always been more concerned with steadily increasing his fortune over time. Because of this strategy, he has been able to withstand the volatility of the market and make intelligent investment choices, all of which have led to his extraordinary level of success.

Case Study 4: J.K. Rowling

The author of the Harry Potter series, J.K. Rowling, is a motivating example of how persistence, goal-setting, and dedication to one's own well-being can lead to an amazing achievement. It is a testimonial to the effectiveness of these routines that she went from receiving assistance to being one of the world's best-selling writers. Her journey began while she was living in poverty.

Rowling's success may be attributed, in large part, to her ability to persevere in the face of adversity. Before her debut novel, Harry Potter and the Sorcerer's Stone, was eventually approved for publication; she had to endure a number of rejections from different publishers. She did not give up on her goal of publication and continued to think that her tale had merit. As a result, she was eventually successful. This tenacity finally paid off, as it resulted in the production of a book series that broke several sales records as well as an entertainment property worth multiple billions of dollars.

Setting goals for herself was also a very important part of Rowling's writing process. She devoted a significant portion of her life to methodically organizing the intricacies of the Harry Potter world, therefore developing a distinct vision for her novels and the ways in which their narratives are related. Because of her sharp mind and laser-like concentration, she was able to bring her concepts to life in a manner that struck a chord with readers all over the globe.

Rowling's dedication to her own health and happiness is another significant reason for her professional accomplishments. She sought help and used writing as a kind of therapy despite the fact that she was dealing with obstacles such as depression and a difficult financial situation. She placed a priority on her mental and physical health. Even when things were tough for her, she was able to keep her creativity and keep writing because of the attention she placed on her well-being.

Case Study 5: Richard Branson

Richard Branson, the creator of the Virgin Group, is a great example of someone who has developed the behaviors of successful and affluent people. He is known for his entrepreneurial spirit. His extraordinary success in a variety of fields is attributable, in part, to his capacity to prioritize networking, take measured risks, and strike a good balance between his personal and professional lives.

The fact that Branson is prepared to take chances has been a major contributor to his level of success. Throughout the course of his career, he has dabbled in a variety of fields with little to no prior expertise, depending instead on his innate instincts and his capacity to pick up new skills on the job. Because he took such a daring approach, he was able to shake up existing markets and come up with novel ideas, which led to the creation of a diversified and prosperous corporate empire.

In addition, Branson's success would not have been possible without his extensive networking. Because of his charming and personable manner, he has been able to establish solid contacts with powerful individuals in a variety of fields, which has contributed to his widespread success. Because of these contacts, new possibilities and partnerships have presented themselves, which has allowed him to further broaden the scope of his enterprises.

Last but not least, one of the most important factors that contributed to Branson's success was his determination to strike a good balance between his profession and his personal life. He has always found time for his family, friends, and personal hobbies, such as kitesurfing and hot air ballooning, despite the fact that he is involved in a large number of commercial endeavors. Branson has been able to maintain his success and fully appreciate the results of his effort because he has discovered how to strike a healthy balance between his professional and personal life.

These case studies of successful people like Elon Musk, Oprah Winfrey, Warren Buffett, and Richard Branson highlight the potential of developing the habits of those who are already successful and affluent. These people have been able to achieve incredible success and have a long-lasting effect on the world as a result of their strong work ethic, dedication to lifelong learning, goal-setting, networking, resilience, financial discipline, and prioritizing of personal well-being.

The significance of each habit in achieving success

The Importance of a Strong Work Ethic in Achieving Success

A solid work ethic is essential to obtaining success because it helps people to pursue their objectives in a consistent manner with the commitment and perseverance necessary to achieve them. A strong work ethic is embodied not just by working hard but also by working intelligently, making sure that both one's time and one's resources are used in the most productive way possible. Successful people are able to optimize their productivity and accomplish their goals in a more effective manner by using strategies such as prioritizing their work based on the relevance and value of the tasks, delegating some of their duties, and using the abilities of others.

The Significance of Lifelong Learning for Success

Learning should continue throughout one's life since it enables people to maintain their relevance and adjust to the ever-evolving environment in which they live. People who engage in continuous learning are better able to gain new information and abilities, which in turn enables them to grab new opportunities and more successfully handle problems. Successful people are able to keep a competitive advantage over their peers and continue to develop on both a personal and a professional level if they remain up to date on the latest developments in their field, technology advances, and best practices. In addition, making a commitment to continue one's education throughout one's life encourages intellectual development and progress, assisting people in developing their ability to think critically and creatively in order to solve issues and develop new ideas.

The Role of Networking in Achieving Success

The ability to create and maintain a strong network of contacts who are able to give support, resources, and opportunities is crucial to an individual's achievement, which is why networking is a necessary habit for success. People that are successful are able to get access to fresh viewpoints, cooperate with others, and grow their influence when they make genuine connections and nurture their relationships. A robust network not only helps people keep informed about the latest advancements in their business but also about the best practices they may use and the possibilities that may be available to them in the future. In addition, people are able to contribute their knowledge and assistance to others via the use of networking, which helps to cultivate an atmosphere of collaborative support and assistance that is to the advantage of all parties concerned.

The Power of Goal-Setting and Planning in Realizing Success

It is essential to create a road to success by setting objectives that are both clear and explicit. People that are successful are adept at expressing their goals, segmenting those goals into segments that are more attainable, and continually assessing and changing their plans to ensure that they are moving in the right direction. Because they have a distinct idea of what it is that they want to do, they are better able to concentrate their energy and resources, which in turn reduces the probability that they will get overwhelmed or lose track of their objectives. In addition, the process of establishing goals and making plans helps to cultivate a feeling of accountability, which in turn encourages people to accept responsibility for their behaviors and choices and to continue to be dedicated to achieving their goals.

The Impact of Time Management and Productivity on Success

Successful individuals have a critical habit that sets them apart, and that is effective time management. They are aware of the worth of their time and are skilled at managing it in such a way as to achieve optimal levels of productivity. Successful people are able to do more in less time and maintain a sustainable level of performance by prioritizing activities, setting limits, and building routines that promote a good work-life balance. In addition, efficient management of one's time helps lower levels of stress and protect against burnout. This ensures that people may continue to perform at their highest levels and pursue their objectives with the utmost concentration and resolve.

The Influence of a Positive Attitude and Resilience on Success

People who are successful are characterized by having a good attitude and being resilient. They are often able to reframe failures as chances for growth and continue to keep their attention fixed on their objectives, even in the face of challenges. Individuals that are successful are able to keep their motivation up and continue to work hard because they have developed a "growth mindset" and are able to retain their optimism even in difficult situations. In addition, having a positive attitude makes it easier to attract opportunities and assistance from others since people are more likely to be attracted to and desire to work with individuals who demonstrate optimism and tenacity.

The Role of Financial Discipline and Planning in Building Wealth

Maintaining a level of wealth over time requires a disciplined approach to one's own finances. Individuals may increase their wealth and attain financial stability by adhering to a budget, saving and investing money prudently, and making choices about their finances after gathering as much information as possible. Establishing a financial plan, establishing budgets, and selecting investments that are in accordance with long-term goals are all essential aspects of practicing financial discipline. In addition, persons who are financially disciplined are better able to build a solid basis for their long-term financial well-being, which helps to ensure that they are able to fulfill their requirements and ambitions during the course of their life.

The Importance of Personal Well-being in Sustaining Success

It has an effect on both a person's physical and mental health, maintaining one's personal well-being is an essential component in achieving and maintaining success. Successful people make taking care of themselves a priority, making certain that they get enough sleep, that they stay active on a regular basis, and that they eat well. They also take care of their mental health by reaching out to others for assistance and participating in activities that enable them to handle stress better and have a positive attitude toward life.

People that are successful are able to keep their energy levels and attention up by taking care of their whole health. This enables them to continue working toward their objectives with the same degree of dedication and fortitude.

In addition, making one's own health and happiness a top priority is an effective way to stave against burnout and cultivate a life that is more balanced and satisfying.

Chapter 2

Breaking Free from the 9-5 Mentality

As more and more individuals demand flexibility and autonomy in their employment, the typical workweek of 9 to 5 is becoming more archaic in today's fast-paced world. To escape the confines of the 9 to 5 mindset, we need to rethink our connection to our jobs, discover what it means to have a healthy work-life balance and investigate other career paths that are in line with our ideals and interests.

Recognizing that the 9-to-5 work schedule is a product of the industrial revolution and was created to optimize efficiency and production during a certain age is one essential component to breaking free from the 9-to-5 mindset. This is because the 9-to-5 work schedule is strict. On the other hand, as a result of developments in technology and the growth of the gig economy, individuals now have more access to flexible work arrangements, which enable them to choose their own working hours and do their jobs from nearly any location.

The adoption of the concept of flexible work schedules is helpful not only for people who are looking to achieve a better work-life balance but also for the businesses that hire such employees. According to a body of academic research, workers who have access to a variety of work-related scheduling options report significantly higher levels of happiness, productivity, and resistance to burnout. In addition, businesses that provide a flexible work environment are more likely to be successful in their recruitment efforts, as an increasing number of working professionals place a high value on maintaining a healthy work-life balance.

Freeing oneself from the confines of the 9-to-5 mindset requires one to also reconsider the conventional concept of achievement. In the past, advancements in one's career, improvements in one's pay, and the amassing of more material belongings were often used as measures of success. On the other hand, as more and more individuals place a greater emphasis on their own pleasure and a sense of purpose in life, the concept of success has evolved to include more abstract notions, such as the capacity to have a beneficial influence on the world and to have good health. Rather than focusing just on climbing the corporate ladder, people may now adopt a more values- and interests-driven approach to achieving success, which enables them to professional fashion lives that are congruent with their identities.

Investigating other avenues of income is yet another strategy for escaping the 9-to-5 mindset and gaining independence. One possibility is to go into a company for oneself or to start a freelance career, both of which enable people to establish their own companies and to work on tasks that are personally significant and satisfying to them. Entrepreneurs and freelancers may create their own schedules, pick their customers, and concentrate on projects that are congruent with their beliefs and interests if they take charge of their professional trajectories and take charge of their careers.

People may break away from the attitude of working a 9-to-5 job by embracing the notion of various income sources. This is in addition to the possibility of starting their own business. This strategy entails earning money through a variety of sources, such as working part-time, providing consulting services, earning passive income from investments, or even making money off of one's hobbies and interests. Individuals may build a more robust and flexible financial condition for themselves by diversifying the sources of income they bring in. This gives them the freedom to explore other career routes and follow their hobbies without being constrained by the confines of a single full-time employee.

In addition, in order to liberate ourselves from the confines of the 9 to 5 mindset, we need to redefine our relationship with work in and of itself. Individuals have the power to adjust their perspective on work so that they see it not as a necessary evil that only offers financial security but rather as an opportunity for development, self-expression, and having a good effect on the world. This shift in perspective may be accomplished by seeing work in this way. People may discover greater purpose and contentment in their employment if they shift their attention to the benefits that come naturally from their work, such as opportunities for self-improvement and a sense of accomplishment.

Analyzing the traditional 9-5 mind-set

The Origins of the 9-5 Mindset

The conventional mentality of working from nine in the morning till five in the afternoon dates back to the time of the industrial revolution when factory employees were expected to adhere to a fixed schedule in order to maintain the highest possible level of output. Because the globe was shifting from an agricultural civilization to one that was dominated by industry and manufacturing, there was an increasing need for a normal workday. This demand grew more pressing as the industrial revolution progressed. This frame of mind was subsequently transferred to the working environment of an office, where it eventually became the norm for white-collar positions as well.

The Impact of the 9-5 Mindset on Society

The mentality of working a 9-to-5 job has had a significant influence on society, not only reshaping the way individuals do their jobs but also their personal life. The establishment of a work-life gap, in which one's personal and professional lives are maintained apart from one another, is one of the most important outcomes of the 9 to 5 workday. This separation may result in many workers not having a healthy balance between their job and personal lives, which can lead to increased stress. The mentality of working a 9 to 5 job has also contributed to the development of a culture that places emphasis on production and efficiency above all else. This emphasis has been a major contributor to economic development; nevertheless, it has also led to employee fatigue and disengagement in the workplace. Because people may have a sense of being constrained by the rigidity of the schedule, the pressure that exists to adapt to the 9 to 5 workday may also result in a loss of creativity and innovation.

The Role of Technology in the 9-5 Mindset

Technology has played a key impact in both the maintenance and the disruption of the mentality of the 9 to 5 workday. On the one hand, technology has made it simpler for businesses to keep track of employee productivity and stick to the traditional Monday through Friday workday. However, technology has also made it possible to have more flexibility in the workplace. This has led to the advent of remote work, telecommuting, and other flexible work arrangements that might pose a threat to the conventional 9 to 5 workday.

The Shift towards a More Flexible Work Environment

In recent years, there has been a rising push away from the conventional mentality of working from 9 to 5, as both employers and workers have become more aware of the advantages of more flexible work arrangements. This transition is the result of a multitude of causes, including shifting cultural norms, an increasing emphasis on work-life balance, and the emergence of the gig economy, among other things.

Companies are starting to realize the value of giving flexible work arrangements in order to recruit and retain top talent as the number of employees who place a higher priority on their own well-being and personal satisfaction increases. According to a body of academic research, workers who have access to a variety of work-related scheduling options report significantly higher levels of happiness, productivity, and resistance to burnout.

The Future of the 9-5 Mindset

Due to the ongoing transformation and development of the contemporary workforce, it is difficult to predict what the future holds for the mentality of working 9 to 5. It is expected that flexible work arrangements will become more widespread as both workers and employers see the advantages of giving greater autonomy and choice in work schedules. This will likely cause flexible work arrangements to become increasingly common. This transition may lead to a rethinking of what it means to have a successful job, with the focus being placed on maintaining a healthy work-life balance, achieving personal satisfaction, and maintaining overall health.

However, it is also likely that the mentality of working from 9 to 5 will continue to be prevalent in particular fields of work and work settings. This is due to the fact that certain businesses may be unwilling to embrace work regulations that are more flexible. It will be vital for people and organizations alike to assess the advantages and downsides of the conventional 9-to-5 mentality and make educated choices about the most suitable work arrangements for their personal needs and objectives as the workforce continues to develop. This will be the case since the workforce is expected to continue to evolve.

The limitations and drawbacks of the 9-5 mentality

Inflexibility and Work-Life Imbalance

The 9 to 5 attitude suffers from a fundamental lack of adaptability, which is one of its most severe drawbacks. Employees sometimes find that they are unable to change their work hours to fit personal duties or hobbies because their employers need them to adhere to a fixed schedule. Because of this rigidity, people may find it difficult to find time outside of their job hours for personal activities and the responsibilities of their families, which may result in a poor work-life balance.

Impact on Employee Health and Well-being

The attitude of working a 9 to 5 shift may also have adverse effects on the health and well-being of the workforce. The emphasis placed on productivity and efficiency often results in a culture of overwork. This is because workers frequently feel driven to put in long hours in order to fulfill deadlines and demonstrate their commitment to the work that they do. Because of this, people may disregard their own self-care and personal needs in favor of their obligations at work, which may lead to increased stress, burnout, and even concerns with their physical health.

Lack of Flexibility for Diverse Needs

The concept of "9 to 5" cannot suit the myriad of requirements that are present in today's workforce. For instance, in order to successfully balance their professional and personal obligations, working parents and those who provide care for others often demand more adaptable working conditions. It's possible that businesses may accidentally alienate some workers and restrict their capacity to contribute effectively to the workplace if they insist on sticking to a tight 9-to-5 schedule.

Stifling Creativity and Innovation

The attitude of working a 9 to 5 job may sometimes be stifling to creative and innovative thinking on the job. A tight timetable does not offer much space for exploration and impromptu activity, both of which are necessary for the development of novel ideas and approaches. The assumption that employees will stick to a set work schedule might make them feel limited, which in turn can hinder their capacity to think creatively and take risks.

Reduced Employee Autonomy

Because workers are expected to adapt to a fixed schedule and set of expectations, the attitude of working from 9 to 5 often restricts the autonomy of employees. Because of this lack of autonomy, workers may feel as if they are unable to make choices about their own work lives, which may lead to feelings of disempowerment and discontent. This, in turn, may lead to reduced levels of engagement as well as lower levels of work satisfaction.

Inefficiencies and Wasted Potential

The attitude of working a 9 to 5 job may lead to inefficiencies and the squandering of potential. Because of this, businesses run the risk of stifling their employees' potential to provide their best work by requiring them to stick to a predetermined work schedule, even if the majority of workers are at their most productive during standard business hours. Employers are able to realize the full potential of their workforce and better capitalize on the distinct advantages and capabilities possessed by each individual member of the workforce when they provide greater leeway for flexible working arrangements.

Alternative perspectives and approaches to work and success

Redefining Success and Work in the Modern World

It is essential to investigate several alternative viewpoints and methods of approaching work and achieving success, especially in light of the fact that the limits and downsides of the conventional "9-to-5 mentality" are becoming increasingly obvious. We can make our work-life experiences more harmonious and gratifying by rethinking what it means to have a profession that is both meaningful and successful. This will allow us to achieve a better balance.

Embracing Work-Life Integration

The idea of integrating one's professional and personal life is one approach that is distinct from the conventional "9 to 5" way of thinking. Work-life integration encourages people to merge their personal and professional lives in a more fluid manner. This is in contrast to the traditional emphasis on delineating clear boundaries between one's personal and professional lives. This strategy emphasizes that one's personal life and one's professional life are interrelated and that striking a balance between the two may result in enhanced happiness and general well-being for the individual.

The Value of Flexibility and Autonomy

Recognizing the benefits of autonomy and flexibility in the workplace is an additional critical component in the process of redefining work and achieving success. Companies may cultivate a culture of trust and empowerment in their workforce by giving workers more say over the schedules and environments in which they do their jobs. This, in turn, may lead to greater levels of work satisfaction, higher levels of engagement, and improved overall performance.

The Importance of Personal Fulfillment and Passion

Putting an emphasis on one's own passions and satisfaction should be a central part of any alternative strategy for achieving success in one's profession. Individuals may find more fulfillment and contentment in their working life if they place a higher priority on doing work that has significance for them and if they match their careers with their beliefs and interests. This change in viewpoint places emphasis on the intrinsic pleasures of labor, such as the opportunity for personal development and self-expression, as well as the opportunity to positively affect the world.

Success beyond Financial Achievement

Changing our conception of what it means to be successful in today's environment requires us to widen our knowledge of what it means to be successful. Other characteristics of success, such as personal development, happiness, and the capacity to have a beneficial influence on the world, are just as significant as monetary success and job progress when it comes to determining one's level of success. Individuals may craft a work path that is more meaningful and enjoyable for themselves by adopting a more comprehensive perspective of what constitutes success.

Exploring Alternative Work Models

It is necessary to investigate alternative work models that challenge the old attitude of working from 9 to 5 so that we may redefine what it means to work and be successful. The following are some examples of these models:

Remote Work and Telecommuting

Employees who participate in remote work or telecommuting have the chance to perform their job duties from any location, giving them more flexibility and autonomy. This form of work not only helps people to better manage their personal and professional duties, but it also enables businesses to tap into a larger pool of talent since physical proximity is less of a limitation in this model.

Flexible Work Arrangements

The amount of control that workers have over their work schedules may be increased by the implementation of flexible work arrangements such as part-time employment, job sharing, or shortened work weeks. Companies are in a better position to meet the varied requirements of their workforce and to foster a healthy work-life balance when they provide a choice of flexible work alternatives to their employees.

Freelancing and Entrepreneurship

Freelancing and entrepreneurship provide people with the opportunity to take charge of their professional trajectories and seek employment that is congruent with their interests, priorities, and ideals. Individuals who go into business for themselves or operate as independent contractors have the ability to choose their own work schedules, pick and select the customers they serve, and concentrate on doing endeavors that they find personally rewarding and significant.

The Gig Economy

The "gig economy," which refers to temporary, contract, and freelance employment, provides people with the option to diversify their income streams and obtain experience working in a number of fields. This possibility is made possible by the gig economy. Without being confined to a single part-time position, people are free to investigate a variety of professional avenues and follow their interests, thanks to the adaptability and liberty made possible by this style of employment.

Creating a Supportive Work Culture

Creating a supportive work culture that places a priority on the health and personal development of employees is a vital component of the process of reinventing work and achieving success. Companies may make their workers feel more appreciated and involved in their job by cultivating an atmosphere that fosters open communication, cooperation, and constant learning.

Chapter 3

Building the Foundation: Small Changes, Big Results

When we are looking to improve ourselves on a personal and professional level, it may be tempting to concentrate on making radical life adjustments and working for lofty objectives. Although using this method might sometimes result in substantial development, it is essential to remember not to underestimate the potential of making even little adjustments in order to produce long-lasting and major outcomes. Building a solid foundation for future success and achieving our goals in a manner that is both more sustainable and more easily controllable may be accomplished if we make continuous, incremental modifications and improvements.

When compared to more significant changes, smaller ones are often simpler to execute and keep up with, which is one of the primary advantages of concentrating on making just little adjustments. For instance, rather than trying to make drastic changes to your diet or exercise regimen all at once, you may begin by making simple tweaks, such as increasing the number of fruits and vegetables you consume at each meal or increasing the amount of time you spend on short walks throughout the day. You may adopt healthier habits over time with the aid of these little modifications, which will provide a firm basis for further development and progress in the future.

Modifying even very small aspects of a work environment may have a big influence on an employee's level of pleasure and overall productivity. Creating a work environment that is both more productive and more pleasurable may be accomplished with the aid of even the smallest of tweaks, such as clearing clutter from your workplace, allotting specific blocks of time for focused work, or instituting frequent breaks to recharge. In addition, firms may find little adjustments that can lead to huge benefits in terms of employee engagement and overall company performance if they cultivate open communication and encourage workers to share their ideas and proposals for development. This encourages employees to share their ideas and suggestions for improvement.

One other benefit of concentrating on making a number of little adjustments is that doing so may assist in the creation of momentum and a positive feedback loop. When we see any kind of advancement, even if it is just in baby steps, it may serve as a source of motivation and motivate us to keep working toward our goals. This feeling of success may assist in developing self-confidence and resilience, making it easier to take on more substantial tasks and barriers when they present themselves in the future.

In addition, even quite little adjustments may have a snowball impact over the course of time. Individually, any modest modification or improvement may not seem to make much of a difference; nevertheless, when added to the effects of other small adjustments, they can have a major impact. This snowball effect may assist in bringing about a change in our lives that is both good and long-lasting, and it can also contribute to our long-term success and sense of contentment.

It is crucial to develop a growth mentality and embrace the notion of constant improvement in order to make the most of the potential that may be unlocked by seemingly little shifts. We may become more open to making modifications to our strategy and refining it as necessary if we learn to perceive difficulties and failures as chances to learn and develop from these experiences. In addition, we may boost both the chance of our success and the likelihood that we will achieve our objectives if we first formulate them such that they are reasonable and doable and then proceed to break them down into more actionable sub-goals.

When one is concentrating on making little adjustments, it is equally important to exercise patience and tenacity. It's possible that we won't see significant results right away, but if we keep making incremental progress toward our goals, we may lay the groundwork for achievements that will endure for a long time. It may be helpful to sustain motivation by celebrating tiny triumphs along the road. This can also reinforce the concept that is making modest improvements can lead to significant benefits.

The concept of incremental changes

The principle behind making changes in stages, or incremental changes, is predicated on the assumption that making relatively few alterations and enhancements on a regular basis might ultimately result in major long-term effects. This strategy runs counter to the prevalent notion that in order to make significant headway, fundamental shifts in one's worldview are required. Individuals and organizations may provide a solid foundation for future achievements and reduce the likelihood of both temporary setbacks and exhaustion by being open to making changes on a more gradual scale.

The Power of Small Steps

One of the most important components of making adjustments gradually is to concentrate on making the shifts in digestible chunks. The incremental method divides major objectives or issues into a series of smaller, more manageable activities rather than trying to attack them head-on as a single entity. This tactic not only makes the process of change less intimidating, but it also enables a more realistic evaluation of both the progress and the success that has been made.

Creating Sustainable Habits

When it comes to developing durable habits and routines, making changes in small, manageable chunks is the most successful strategy. We may avoid the resistance and pain that often follow more dramatic changes in our lives by gradually bringing new habits and activities into our everyday routines. This allows us to take advantage of the opportunities presented by these changes. This strategy may be very useful when it comes to sustaining motivation and consistency over time, as it enables a more gradual adaptation to new habits and routines, which can be extremely effective in achieving these goals.

The Compound Effect

The compound effect, which is the cumulative influence of tiny improvements over the course of time, is an integral part of incremental changes and one of its fundamental aspects. When seen alone, some adjustments may not seem to have much of an impact, yet, when taken together, they might have a considerable impact. This concept emphasizes the need for consistency and perseverance in the pursuit of personal and professional progress. Even apparently, little alterations may have a profound influence when done consistently over time, and this principle demonstrates how important it is to maintain this consistency and tenacity.

Applying Incremental Changes in the Workplace

In the workplace, adjustments that are made gradually may be very advantageous since they make the process of progress and growth more controllable and durable. Organizations are able to establish a culture of continuous improvement that is beneficial to the growth of their employees as well as the overall success of the firm if they place emphasis on making incremental changes and improvements.

Continuous Improvement and Innovation

One of the most important ways that little adjustments may be applied in the workplace is in the form of the idea of continuous improvement and innovation. Organizations are able to keep one step ahead of the competition and adjust more successfully to shifts in the market if they cultivate a culture that encourages people to continuously seek out chances to further their education and professional development. Because workers are given the impression that they have the ability to make a contribution to the continued success of the organization, this strategy may also serve to enhance employee engagement and job happiness.

Employee Development and Training

Changes made on a more incremental scale may also play an important part in the growth and training of employees. Employees have a better chance of feeling confident and competent in their talents if the process of acquiring new skills and developing existing ones is broken down into smaller, more manageable stages. Individuals are able to see the progress they are making and have a better understanding of the route to mastery as a result of this strategy, which may also assist in lessening the emotions of being overwhelmed and frustrated.

Performance Management and Goal Setting

The strategy of doing things one step at a time may also be used inside an organization for performance management and the establishment of goals. Employees may develop a better knowledge of their goals and the actions that must be taken to reach them if the goals they establish for themselves are attainable and practical and if the goals are broken down into more manageable stages. As a result of this approach, people are better able to monitor their progress and celebrate their victories along the way, which may also assist in contributing to the development of a work atmosphere that is more encouraging and uplifting.

The Role of Incremental Changes in Personal Growth

In addition to the positive effects they have on performance in the workplace, incremental improvements may also have a significant impact on an individual's capacity for development and self-improvement. Individuals may establish a more manageable and sustainable route to success in different aspects of their life if they concentrate on taking baby steps that are easily attainable for them.

Physical Health and Wellness

When it comes to an individual's physical health and well-being, making little adjustments over time may be particularly useful in terms of assisting them in the formation of long-lasting, good habits. Individuals may lower the risk of burnout and enhance the possibility that they will sustain these behaviors over the long term if they start new exercise routines, dietary modifications, or self-care activities gradually and introduce them one at a time.

Emotional and Mental Well-being

The strategy of doing things one step at a time may also be used in an effort to improve one's emotional and mental health. Individuals may progressively build resilience, establish good coping strategies, and create a more positive mentality if they concentrate their efforts on taking baby steps that are easily doable. Taking this approach paves the way for a personal development and emotional well-being journey that is not only more sustainable but also more helpful.

Financial Stability and Growth

When it comes to one's personal finances, making little adjustments over time may be an important factor in attaining both financial stability and development. Individuals may construct a solid financial foundation and make progress toward their long-term financial objectives by methodically putting into practice budgeting tactics, saving routines, and appropriate spending behaviors in a step-by-step manner.

Strategies for incorporating small habits into daily life

It is crucial to establish techniques for adopting little habits into our everyday lives if we are going to harness the potential that may be unlocked by making changes over time, one step at a time. The following are some concrete strategies that might assist people and organizations in embracing and maintaining gradual change.

Start with a Clear Goal

Establishing a goal that is crystal clear and well-defined is the first thing that needs to be done in order to successfully integrate little habits into everyday life. Individuals are able to construct a focused strategy for making incremental adjustments that match their aims if they first determine the intended result, then define what constitutes success in that endeavor.

Break Goals into Smaller Tasks

After a specific objective has been identified, the next step is to subdivide it into a series of progressively more achievable subtasks. Individuals may build a plan that is more practical and attainable for the purpose of making incremental changes in their day-to-day life if they divide the bigger aim into smaller stages and work backward from there.

Establish a Routine

To effectively incorporate new, smaller habits into one's everyday life, it is essential to first establish a steady routine for oneself. Individuals may more readily incorporate new behaviors into their preexisting schedules and routines if they designate certain times and locations for the implementation of their new habits.

Monitor Progress and Adjust Accordingly

Maintaining gradual improvements requires a number of steps, one of which is the consistent monitoring of progress and the implementation of necessary modifications. Individuals may better identify areas for growth and adapt their approach to better support their objectives if they keep a record of both their accomplishments and their failures.

Celebrate Small Wins

Recognizing and applauding one's progress toward a goal, no matter how little, is a strong motivator that may help one keep momentum and remain dedicated to making incremental adjustments. Individuals may increase their self-confidence and perpetuate the concept that even the smallest behaviors can lead to huge outcomes if they acknowledge even their little successes.

Be Patient and Persistent

When trying to incorporate smaller habits into one's daily routine, patience and tenacity are two traits that are very necessary to cultivate. Individuals may gradually construct a solid foundation for long-term success by constantly making modest adjustments to their behaviors, even though the first changes may not seem to have any significant impact.

How these small habits compound over time

The power of seemingly little behaviors rests in their capacity to accumulate over time and have major and long-lasting effects. The process of compounding entails the slow accumulation of development via the constant practice of smaller habits that are then built upon. This process takes place over time. Each little adjustment leads to a bigger, more significant modification over time, which may have a significant impact on an individual's personal and professional life if it is allowed to go unchecked.

Consistency is one of the most important variables that play a role in the development of tiny habits over time.

Individuals enhance the probability that a behavior will become entrenched and automatic when they make a commitment to exercising a new habit or making a tiny modification on a regular basis. This increases the likelihood that the habit will be beneficial. As the routine becomes more second nature, it has the potential to act as a platform upon which new changes may be built, so initiating a cycle of constructive expansion and improvement.

Take, for instance, the endeavor of establishing a schedule for regular physical activity as an example. A person may start by committing to walking for ten minutes every day. As time goes on and this pattern becomes more ingrained in their lives, it is possible that they may progressively extend the length of their walks and raise the intensity of their walking, ultimately including new types of physical activity into their routine. They may feel encouraged to take on even larger challenges as their fitness levels increase and as they get more confidence in their skills. For example, they may become interested in taking part in a race or joining a sports team as their fitness levels progress. An apparently modest practice, like walking for 30 minutes every day, may lead to considerable changes in one's physical fitness and general well-being because of the compounding effect.

The idea of self-reinforcement is another significant component that plays a significant role in the compounding impact that is caused by insignificant behaviors. Individuals are more likely to feel inspired to continue their efforts and build upon their accomplishments when they begin to see progress and experience the advantages of their new habits. This is because seeing progress and experiencing the benefits of their new habits go hand in hand. This feeling of satisfaction has the potential to generate a positive feedback loop in which the drive to attain even larger accomplishments is fueled by each successive minor victory.

For example, if an individual is looking to improve their own financial situation, they may begin by implementing a very little adjustment, such as setting aside a smaller portion of their monthly salary to save. They may feel inspired to raise the amount they save each month or investigate alternative ways for managing their money, such as investing or lowering their debt, as they see their savings account balance improve over time. These seemingly little behaviors, when added up over time, have the potential to have a materially favorable influence on their financial security and the achievement of their long-term financial objectives.

In the sphere of personal and professional relationships, the influence of tiny behaviors that are repeated over time may also be demonstrated to have a compounding effect. Individuals are able to progressively create deeper relationships with others around them if they routinely engage in modest acts of kindness, demonstrate empathy, and engage in active listening. When these behaviors become more second nature, they have the potential to provide the groundwork for trust and mutual support, which in turn may lead to relationships that are more satisfying and meaningful.

Chapter 4

Cultivating the Success Mind-set

The development of a success mentality is an important component of both personal and professional development, as it has the potential to affect our ideas, actions, and, eventually, our accomplishments. A success mentality is defined by an optimistic perspective, confidence that one is able to overcome problems, and a dedication to ongoing progress. These are the three pillars of a growth mindset. The development of this attitude enables people to realize their greatest potential and bring about changes in their lives that are both long-lasting and significant.

The conviction that one is capable of acquiring new skills and expanding one's knowledge is an essential component of a mentality that is geared toward achievement.

The acceptance of the power that comes from establishing goals is another essential component of the success mentality. Individuals may establish a road map for their own achievement and keep their drive in the face of challenges if they set objectives that are crystal clear, very detailed, and easily attainable. In addition, people may create momentum and enjoy a sense of achievement as they advance toward their goals if they break down big goals into smaller activities that are easier to handle.

Setting goals and developing efficient strategies for managing time are both essential components of developing a mentality that is geared toward achieving success. People are able to boost their productivity and feel more in control of their day-to-day life if they organize their responsibilities according to their level of importance, steer clear of activities that divert their attention, and set up a dedicated time for in-depth work. In addition, people are able to continuously develop their approach and maximize their performance by routinely analyzing and making adjustments to the tactics they use to manage their time.

The cultivation of a mentality for success also requires the development of self-awareness as a vital component. Individuals are able to make choices that are more informed and better connect their actions with their objectives when they have a clear awareness of their own beliefs, as well as their strengths and shortcomings. Individuals may also cultivate better confidence in their talents and build a more optimistic view of life if they are able to recognize and challenge the self-limiting beliefs and negative thinking patterns that they have developed through time.

Building a solid support network is another essential component of a successful mentality. It is possible to cultivate an atmosphere that is mutually encouraging and inspirational if one surrounds themselves with good influences and persons who have similar values and goals. Building relationships with those who share a dedication to one's personal and professional development may be accomplished in a number of ways, including but not limited to networking, joining clubs or professional groups, and seeking out mentors.

The adoption of the idea of continuous education throughout one's life is yet another crucial component of the attitude of a successful person. Individuals may remain adaptive and keep a competitive advantage in both their personal and professional life if they continue to seek out new information and abilities on a consistent basis. Expanding one's knowledge and gaining new abilities may be accomplished in a number of different ways, including taking part in workshops, reading books, attending seminars, and taking online courses.

The last step in developing a mentality for success is to cultivate self-compassion and strike a good balance between one's professional and personal life. Even if it is critical to be tenacious and devoted to the accomplishment of one's objectives, it is equally necessary to acknowledge the need for periods of rest, relaxation, and self-care. Individuals are able to preserve their mental and emotional well-being and, ultimately, their potential for achievement when they prioritize self-care and establish clear boundaries in their lives.

The importance of mind-set in achieving success and wealth

Embracing Challenges and Overcoming Failures

People who have a growth mentality see obstacles as chances to learn and expand their knowledge and skills. They are aware that the extent to which they succeed or fail is not a measure of their inherent capabilities but rather a crucial component of the learning process. They are able to cultivate resiliency and persistence as a result of this mentality, which are crucial attributes for obtaining success and accumulating riches. People who adopt a growth mindset are more likely to have major success in their personal and professional life. They do this by continually testing their limits and learning from the lessons that come from their failures.

Continuous Learning and Adaptability

The idea that there is always potential for progress is ingrained in those who have a growth mentality. People who have this mentality are dedicated to continuing their education throughout their lives and are receptive to criticism, which enables them to pinpoint areas in which they may acquire new abilities or improve upon those they already possess. In today's fast-changing world, when adaptation and creativity are essential to gaining success and riches, this process of ongoing education is more important than ever before. Individuals that have a growth mentality may better position themselves for job promotion and financial success if they remain current with new information, trends, and technology. This can be accomplished by keeping abreast of these developments.

The Pitfalls of a Fixed Mindset and Its Impact on Success and Wealth

On the other side, one might be said to have a fixed mentality if one holds the notion that intelligence and talents are permanent traits that cannot be greatly altered or improved upon. Because of this perspective, people may not fully achieve their potential or be as adaptive to changes in their environment, both of which may be obstacles on the path to earning success and prosperity.

Limiting Beliefs and Fear of Failure

People who have a fixed mentality often have restrictive views about their own capabilities and potential, which might prevent them from pursuing lofty objectives or taking risks. They may shun challenges because they think that their talents are fixed and cannot be modified, which may cause them to feel vulnerable to humiliation or failure. This fear of failing may be detrimental to their growth because it reduces the likelihood that they will cultivate the resilience and tenacity required to overcome the challenges and disappointments that lie ahead on the road to success and financial well-being.

Complacency and Lack of Growth

A fixed mentality may cause people to become self-satisfied because they may incorrectly believe that their existing skills and knowledge are enough to achieve their goals. This notion might hamper a person's desire to learn new things and adapt, both of which are essential in a world that is always changing. Individuals who have a fixed mentality, on the other hand, are more likely to find themselves sliding behind their contemporaries and rivals, which, in the end, will restrict their prospects for professional development and increased income.

Tips and exercises for developing a success mind-set

Having a mentality that is geared toward success is critical to one's ability to achieve both personal and professional objectives. It is the factor that differentiates those who are successful from others who struggle to find their footing in a world that is more competitive. This book will give you helpful strategies and exercises to establish and maintain a mentality that is focused on growth, optimism, and accomplishment. These will help you reach your goals more effectively. You will be able to reach your full potential and put yourself in a position to be successful if you put these methods into action.

The Power of Positive Thinking

Accepting the power that positive thought may have is one of the most important components of creating a mindset for success. It's simple for negative thoughts to get out of hand, and that might keep you from doing the things you set out to do. As a result, it is essential to train oneself to have a positive attitude toward life and to concentrate on finding solutions rather than finding problems.

To get started, take stock of the negative ideas that pop into your head on a regular basis. Put them in writing, and then rephrase them such that they are positive remarks. Alternately, "I'll never be able to do this" might be rephrased as "I can learn and improve with practice." Maintaining a good outlook throughout the day requires frequent repetition of these fresh affirmations.

Visualize Success

When it comes to achieving one's goals, visualization is a very useful technique. You may better prepare your brain for the success you want if you conjure up a vision in your head of what you want the end result to be. A visualization is a useful tool for maintaining attention and keeping oneself motivated while working toward one's objectives.

Dedicate ten minutes of your time every day to seeing yourself successfully accomplishing your objectives. Put your eyes out and try to conjure up the specifics, such as the sensation of having accomplished something, the responses of others around you, and the setting in which you found yourself. Create as vivid a picture as you can from this mental image.

Set Clear and Achievable Goals

Setting goals is a vital part of developing a mentality that is geared toward success. It lays forth a plan for you to follow, guaranteeing that your efforts will be focused on making substantial progress in the right direction. Nevertheless, it is essential to establish objectives that are crystal clear, detailed, and attainable and that are in line with your beliefs and desires.

Make a list of your long-term objectives, and then divide each of those objectives into shorter-term objectives that are more doable. Write down the actions you need to do in order to accomplish each of your goals, as well as any possible roadblocks and the solutions you have in mind to overcome them.

Embrace a Growth Mindset

The conviction that one may continually improve their capabilities via the application of effort and the acquisition of new knowledge is known as a growth mindset. This attitude helps you to perceive obstacles as chances to progress, and it pushes you to continue in spite of setbacks by encouraging you to view challenges as opportunities to grow.

Consider your experiences from the past, and try to pick out specific occasions in which you demonstrated a development mentality. Recognize the value of the experiences you've had and how they've influenced your growth as an individual. Make use of these realizations to adopt a development attitude in approaching future obstacles.

Cultivate Resilience

The capacity to recover quickly and effectively from adversity is a key component of resilience. The cultivation of resilience is an essential component of sustaining a success mentality because it helps you to persevere in the face of adversity and keep moving forward toward the accomplishment of your objectives.

Determine a recent setback or failure, and then conduct an analysis of the variables that led to that setback or failure. Find out what you may have done better, and use this knowledge to improve your performance in similar circumstances in the future. The more you can train yourself to see failures as chances for growth and improvement, the better off you will be.

Surround Yourself with Positivity

Your frame of mind is significantly influenced by the company you keep. Who you keep in your inner circle matters. Your drive and sense of self-confidence will increase when you surround yourself with upbeat, encouraging people, but your advancement may be stymied if you hang around with negative influences.

Take stock of your present social circle and pinpoint the people in it who make a positive contribution to your development and progress. You should make an effort to spend more time with the individuals who support your goals and objectives, and you should remove yourself from the ones who do not.

Develop Self-Discipline

A mentality that is geared toward achievement relies heavily on the practice of self-control. It is the capacity to avoid becoming sidetracked, to keep one's concentration, and to put one's long-term objectives ahead of short-term pleasures or comfort. The cultivation of self-discipline makes it more likely that you will remain devoted to achieving your goals, even in the face of challenges.

Addressing common mental barriers and how to overcome them

The presence of mental barriers may be a substantial impediment to one's growth and can prevent one from accomplishing their objectives. You may create the route for your own personal and professional success by facing these challenges head-on and gaining the skills necessary to overcome them. This content will provide you with the skills and tactics you need to overcome common mental obstacles and unlock your entire potential so that you may reach your maximum potential.

Recognizing Limiting Beliefs

Negative ideas that limit your potential and prevent you from achieving your objectives are examples of limiting beliefs. These ideas are often the result of previous experiences, the expectations of society, or internalized self-doubt. The first step in overcoming these ideas is to become aware of them and then question them.

Think about the beliefs that hold you back the most and write them down. Determine the origin of each belief and think about whether or not it is based on accurate observation or a warped interpretation of the world. You should start to question and reinterpret these ideas by using phrases that are positive and powerful.

Overcoming the Fear of Failure

Fear of falling short of one's goals is a prevalent mental obstacle that may impede forward movement. This dread is often brought on by a desire to be flawless, to have high expectations, or to shield oneself from failure. You may learn to accept failure as a chance to learn and better if you first come to terms with the fact that it is an inevitable component of the maturation process.

Consider your previous setbacks and the valuable lessons you were able to glean from each event. Utilize these realizations to cultivate a better attitude toward failure, seeing it instead as a necessary step on the path to achievement.

Combatting Procrastination

Postponing activities or making choices is the act of procrastination, which often leads to higher stress levels and decreased levels of productivity. To be successful in overcoming procrastination, one must first have an awareness of the factors that contribute to it and then put into practice tactics that boost motivation and help one to stay focused.

Determine the activities that you have a habit of putting off and the reasons that lie behind your avoidance of them. Create a plan of action to address these underlying issues, which may involve breaking down activities into smaller pieces, creating deadlines, or putting up a reward system for successfully completing chores.

Managing Impostor Syndrome

The impostor syndrome is the continuous idea that you are unworthy of your accomplishments and will ultimately be found to as a phony. This belief might make you feel as if you are a fraud right now. This mental barrier may lead to feelings of self-doubt as well as worry and a reduction in one's self-confidence. Recognizing your own successes and coming to terms with your own value are necessary steps in overcoming imposter syndrome.

Create a list of the accomplishments, talents, and qualities that you possess. You should routinely remind yourself that you have worked hard for your accomplishment by reviewing this list. It is important to develop the habit of graciously receiving comments and appreciation without attributing your successes to chance or other outside influences.

Building Self-Confidence

The feeling that one is capable and deserving of anything is the foundation of self-confidence. Because of the impact it has on your drive, resilience, and willingness to take risks, it is an essential component of a success mentality. Developing one's self-confidence is a process that involves constant work and practice.

Keep in mind your successes and areas of strength, and look for opportunities to participate in pursuits that will highlight your abilities. Put your self-confidence to the test by challenging yourself with novel experiences, and gradually put yourself in environments that will put your self-assurance to the test. You may strengthen your sense of self-assurance over time by regularly challenging yourself to overcome your anxieties and concerns.

Handling Stress and Anxiety

Both stress and anxiety are typical mental obstacles that may have a severe influence on a person's performance as well as their overall health and well-being. Maintaining a success mentality and being able to effectively manage these emotions is key to conquering challenges that may arise.

Create a toolbox of ways to relieve stress, such as meditating on the present moment, doing deep breathing exercises, or engaging in physical activity. You may better manage your stress and anxiety by incorporating these routines into your regular routine and drawing on them when required.

Developing Emotional Intelligence

The capacity to identify, comprehend, and effectively regulate one's own emotions, as well as the emotions of others, is referred to as emotional intelligence (EQ). When it comes to negotiating interpersonal interactions and overcoming mental hurdles, it is an essential talent to have.

Maintaining self-awareness requires constant introspection on one's feelings and the ways in which those feelings influence one's behavior. You may cultivate empathy by taking into account the viewpoints and emotions of other people, and you can refine your abilities in emotional regulation by learning how to moderate your own emotional reactions when confronted with difficult circumstances.

Embracing a Balanced Perspective

Recognizing both the good and negative sides of your life and the experiences you've had is an important step in developing a more balanced view. Keeping a balanced view helps prevent negative ideas from dominating your thinking and allows you to tackle challenges with a feeling of optimism and resilience. This is because maintaining a balanced outlook helps prevent negative thoughts from dominating your mindset.

When confronted with a difficult issue, you should make a concerted effort to determine both the advantageous and disadvantageous aspects of the circumstance. Consider the possible positive outcomes, possibilities, and personal development that may result from the experience, and reassure yourself that momentary obstacles are something that can be surmounted.

Cultivating Patience and Perseverance

As a result of the fact that it is seldom accomplished immediately, patience and endurance are often required to achieve success. You'll be able to keep your drive and dedication to your objectives alive and well if you cultivate these traits. This will be true even in the face of obstacles and delays.

Establish reasonable goals for your future advancement and acknowledge that achieving achievement may take some time. When you are confronted with challenges, it is important to keep your long-term objectives and the significance of maintaining your path in mind. By dividing projects up into more manageable chunks and keeping track of your progress along the way, you may develop the traits of patience and persistence.

Chapter 5

The Power of Consistency

In the pursuit of success and personal development, it is common practice to disregard the power that consistency has. Consistency is a useful tool for serving as a reminder of the significance of making a consistent, persistent effort in a society that is saturated with immediate satisfaction and short solutions. The building of habits, the successful completion of objectives, and the acquisition of new abilities are all directly attributable to one's level of consistency. Unlocking your potential and making considerable progress in a variety of facets of your life may be accomplished by developing an awareness of the power of consistency and making effective use of it.

The ability of consistency to play a part in the development of habits is one of its key advantages. The patterns of behavior and activities that we engage in on a regular basis are referred to as habits. We eventually change acts that we engage in consistently over time into habits that demand minimum conscious effort on our part when we engage in these actions. This procedure releases mental resources, which enables us to concentrate on other elements of our lives while continuing to make forward toward the achievement of our objectives.

Consider, for illustration purposes, the steps involved in acquiring the ability to play an instrument. When you first start practicing, you may find that it is difficult and requires a substantial amount of mental energy. However, if you practice your instrument regularly, playing it will eventually become second nature to you. This will free up the musician to concentrate on honing their skill and discovering new ways to express their creativity.

In the pursuit of one's personal and professional objectives, consistency is another quality that is very necessary. You may maintain forward momentum in the face of obstacles and failures if you take persistent activity toward achieving your goals. This will produce momentum that will drive you ahead. This momentum is essential to keeping your motivation up and ensuring that you do not stray from the path that will lead you to achieve your objectives.

Take, for example, the situation of a person who wants to reduce their body fat percentage. They should be able to make moderate progress toward their objective if they adhere to a balanced diet and an exercise plan on a regular basis. In contrast, someone who just sometimes participates in healthy activities may find it difficult to keep the momentum going and produce outcomes that are long-lasting.

The idea of compound effects is another illustration of the strength that comes from maintaining consistency. When you do the same steps on a regular basis over a period of time, the advantages you get will eventually add up to exponential growth and development. This principle is analogous to the notion of compound interest, which is used in the field of finance. According to this theory, modest investments that are maintained over time result in astronomical returns owing to the accumulation of interest. When it comes to one's own development, the cumulative effects of exerting persistent effort may lead to major advances in one's abilities, habits, and accomplishments.

For example, devoting just half an hour each day to the study of a new language may not seem to be very much at first glance. However, if you put in constant work over a period of time, you will eventually make significant progress and become proficient in the target language. The cumulative consequences of consistency are potent, and they apply to practically every facet of one's life, from maintaining one's physical condition to advancing one's professional standing.

Creating coherence in your life calls for self-discipline, dedication, and an unmistakable awareness of the direction you want to take it. Determine the areas in which you feel you have the most room for development or advancement as a starting point. Divide each of these objectives into a series of smaller, more doable activities that you may continue to work on a daily basis. You will generate forward momentum and cultivate a feeling of success if you take baby moves in the direction of achieving your goals.

The importance of consistency in maintaining and growing habits

When it comes to the development, upkeep, and expansion of habits, consistency is essential. It is the secret to unlocking long-term success in both one's professional and one's personal endeavors. You may harness the power of habits to alter your life in meaningful and good ways if you grasp the significance of maintaining consistency throughout the process of developing and cultivating habits. This all-encompassing book will dig into the relevance of consistency and give helpful insights into how to use it to maintain and strengthen habits over time.

The Science behind Consistency and Habit Formation

The science behind how our brains create and keep habits is where the concept of consistency got its start. Repetition and positive reinforcement are the fundamental tenets upon which the basal ganglia, the part of the brain that is accountable for the development of habits is based. When we participate in the same action over and over again, we develop brain connections, which eventually result in the formation of a habit loop. The trigger, the routine, and the reward that are all part of this habit loop work together to produce an automatic reaction that takes very little conscious effort. This habit loop is strengthened when we continuously repeat an activity; as a result, the behavior becomes more established and is simpler to sustain over the course of time.

Building Momentum through Consistency

When it comes to the formation of habits and the upkeep of those habits, consistency is a great instrument for developing momentum. When you participate in the same action on a continuous basis, you develop a feeling of progression and success for yourself. This positive feedback loop functions as motivation, fuelling your desire to repeat the activity and build the habit further. Maintaining motivation and pushing through problems, setbacks, or plateaus that may happen throughout the process of habit development requires momentum like no other. Momentum is essential for this.

Overcoming Challenges with Consistency

It is impossible to avoid difficulties in life or the process of forming habits. Because it enables you to stay dedicated to your routines in spite of disruptions, consistency is an essential component in the process of conquering these challenges. When you are confronted with obstacles, maintaining regular conduct serves as an anchor, which provides stability and grounds your activities. You convey a strong message to yourself and others about your tenacity, perseverance, and devotion to your objectives when you maintain consistency. This message is about your commitment to achieving those goals.

Adapting and Evolving Habits through Consistency

It's possible that as you advance in your personal and professional life, you'll find that some habits need to be adjusted in order to account for shifting circumstances, priorities, or objectives. Maintaining a consistent routine throughout the process of modifying and improving your routine so that it better meets your requirements is vital. If you regularly assess your routines and make any required improvements, you can guarantee that they will continue to contribute to your development and success in the future. Fostering an agile mentality, which enables you to adapt and prosper in the face of change, requires consistent monitoring and refinement of your behaviors.

Fostering Accountability with Consistency

In order to encourage responsibility, consistency is another factor that plays a very important function. When you participate in behavior in a manner that is consistent throughout time, you hold yourself responsible for your objectives and strengthen your dedication to accomplishing them. Sharing your objectives with other people adds an additional dimension of accountability to the process, which may help you develop a deeper feeling of personal responsibility. Not only are you holding yourself responsible when you demonstrate your devotion to your routines in a regular manner, but you are also motivating people around you to do the same thing.

Cultivating Long-term Success through Consistency

The potential of consistency to foster long-term success is the ultimate factor that determines the significance of sustaining and expanding habits consistently. You may construct a solid basis for both your personal and professional development by persistently rewarding desirable actions and altering routines in response to changing circumstances. Maintaining a consistent approach guarantees that the habits you've developed continue to advance you toward your objectives and help you realize your full potential.

Strategies for staying consistent and motivated

It is essential to keep one's motivation and consistency high in order to accomplish one's personal and professional objectives. These two components serve as the basis for the creation of habits, which is essential for both personal development and professional achievement. This in-depth book will give you six critical tactics for maintaining consistency and motivation in your activities, so assisting you in unlocking your full potential and achieving achievements that will endure.

Establish Clear Goals and Priorities

It is necessary to create clear objectives and priorities in order to keep one's consistency and motivation at a high level. Your activities will be directed, giving you a sense of purpose, and you'll be able to keep your attention on what really counts when you have clear goals to work toward. When it comes to goal-setting, you should adhere to the SMART criteria, which are as follows: specific, measurable, attainable, relevant, and time-bound. This strategy will guarantee that your objectives are distinct, attainable, and congruent with both your values and your desires. You can keep your motivation up and make sure that your activities are in line with the vision you have for the future if you regularly strive towards your priorities.

Develop a Structured Routine

It is very necessary to have a set routine in order to keep one's consistency and drive. You may create a feeling of consistency and predictability in your day by structuring it around your priorities, which will make it easier for you to remain on track and complete the things you have set out to do. Create a routine for yourself that includes time for your most critical duties, as well as time for self-care, relaxation, and social events. This routine may be on a daily or weekly basis. Keeping your motivation up, avoiding burnout, and making sure you're always making progress toward your goals are all things that can be accomplished by building a routine that's just right for you.

Break Tasks into Manageable Steps

A great tactic for maintaining consistency and keeping motivated is to divide activities into smaller, more achievable chunks. It's easy to become discouraged and put off starting or completing challenging projects when they're too big or too complicated. You may alleviate some of the mental strain and make progress more doable if you break down the work at hand into more reasonable and concise chunks. In addition, finishing each stage gives you a feeling of success and progress, which in turn increases your drive and helps you move closer to achieving your objectives.

Monitor Progress and Celebrate Success

Monitoring your progress and recognizing your accomplishments are two of the most important things you can do to keep yourself motivated and consistent. Assess your progress toward your objectives on a regular basis, taking time to think about the actions you've already taken and the challenges you've already conquered. You may strengthen your drive and keep a feeling of momentum going by giving yourself credit for your accomplishments, regardless of how little they may be. You may want to think about establishing milestones along the road and celebrating them as they are attained; this will serve as a concrete reminder of your progress and commitment.

Cultivate a Support Network

It is quite helpful to have a solid support network in order to keep one's consistency and drive. Put yourself in the company of people who not only share your beliefs, objectives, and ambitions but also are able to support you, give you advice, and hold you accountable for your actions. You can keep your motivation up, manage obstacles, and get helpful feedback on your progress if you frequently interact with the people who make up your support network. In addition, the mutual support and inspiration that may be gained from one's network can help drive one toward achievement while also helping others.

Cultivate Resilience and Adaptability

In order to keep one's composure and one's motivation high in the face of obstacles and failures, it is necessary to possess the traits of resilience and adaptability. Foster resiliency in yourself by reinterpreting failures as chances for personal development and education and by cultivating a growth mindset that places emphasis on making an effort, making progress, and being persistent. Embrace flexibility by having a flexible viewpoint, changing your techniques and behaviors as necessary, and being open to new experiences. You will be able to maintain your consistency and motivation if you cultivate these traits. This will be true even when you are confronted with challenges and uncertainties.

The benefits of consistency in achieving long-term success

In both one's personal life and one's professional life, consistency is a tremendous force that drives achievement. It is essential for the development of habits, the upkeep of motivation, and the triumph over adversities. The advantages of consistency are not limited to short-term accomplishments; rather, it is an essential factor in both long-term success and individual development. This all-encompassing book will examine six significant advantages of consistency, highlighting how this essential component may drive you toward long-term success in your activities.

Strengthening Habits and Routines

One of the most important advantages of maintaining a consistent approach is the function that it plays in solidifying habits and routines. Our actions, ideas, and behaviors are all shaped by our habits, making them the bedrock around which our everyday lives are built. By doing the same things over and over again, we strengthen the neural circuits that underlie habits in our brains, which in turn makes the behavior more instinctive and requires less conscious effort. Because of this process, we are able to continue making forward toward our objectives while simultaneously liberating brain capacity for use in other endeavors. The development of stable habits and routines provides a strong basis for both long-term success and personal development.

Cultivating Discipline and Self-control

Maintaining consistency in one's behavior is an effective way to establish discipline and self-control, both of which are necessary attributes for attaining sustained success. By following a routine or working towards a goal in a regular manner, we build the capacity to resist distractions and properly prioritize our activities. Because of our self-discipline, we are able to maintain our concentration on our goals even when we are confronted with obstacles or temptations that may slow down our progress. This enhanced self-control, when practiced over time, promotes resilience and determination, which are essential components for attaining long-term success.

Building Confidence and Self-efficacy

Building our confidence and sense of self-efficacy is another benefit that comes from being consistent in the acts that we do. The concept of self-efficacy relates to the confidence that we have in our own capabilities to complete tasks and realize our ambitions. The more we put in the effort to achieve our goals and see that we are making headway, the more self-assured we become about our capabilities. This heightened sense of self-confidence serves as fuel for motivation and inspires us to establish and work toward objectives that are even loftier, which in turn creates a positive cycle of development and accomplishment.

Establishing Credibility and Trust

When it comes to building credibility and trust in both professional and personal relationships, consistency is one of the most important factors. Behaving in a manner that is consistent indicates commitment, dependability, and devotion, all of which are traits that other people appreciate and cherish. We develop a reputation of dependability and expertise by reliably following through on our commitments, observing deadlines, and performing at a high level across all of our endeavors. This credibility helps to cultivate good connections, opens doors to new possibilities, and adds to the success that we enjoy in many facets of our life over the long run.

Creating Momentum and Sustaining Progress

When it comes to generating momentum and maintaining forward movement toward long-term objectives, consistency is very necessary. We can develop a sensation of forward momentum that helps us get closer to achieving our goals if we take action on a continuous basis. This momentum is helpful in maintaining motivation, which in turn makes it easier to overcome problems and setbacks that may occur along the route. By maintaining progress via persistent work, we guarantee that our objectives will continue to be within our grasp and that the accomplishments we make will be long-lasting and significant.

Facilitating Continuous Improvement and Growth

Maintaining a consistent approach is essential to fostering both continual progress and personal development. We are able to discover areas of strength and weakness by continuously analyzing our routines, actions, and outcomes. This provides us with the opportunity to enhance our strategy and make any required modifications. This never-ending cycle of introspection and self-improvement helps to guarantee that our routines and approaches continue to be useful and are in line with our objectives. We may unleash our full potential and lay the groundwork for long-term success if we accept consistency as a tool for ongoing development and use it as our guiding principle.

Chapter 6

Networking and Relationship Building

Building relationships and engaging in other forms of networking are fundamental to one's career as well as personal success. They include forming and sustaining relationships with other people, as well as building mutual understanding and establishing trust among one another. These interactions have the potential to facilitate the development of new possibilities, important insights, and personal progress for each party involved. The time and energy that you put into cultivating connections and networking may pay off in a variety of different ways, including the growth of your profession as well as the enrichment of your personal life.

Being proactive in finding new contacts to network with is one of the most important components of the practice of networking. Attending events, becoming a member of groups or organizations, and engaging in conversations within online communities are all examples of this. Your visibility will improve, and possibilities for meaningful connections will present themselves, provided that you actively engage with other people. It is also vital to approach the process of networking with a mentality that is one of curiosity and openness since having a genuine interest in the experiences and perspectives of others encourages the development of stronger ties.

Networking and connection building are two activities that can only be successful when effective communication is present. The ability to construct a solid foundation for meaningful interactions requires essential abilities such as attentive listening and the expression of empathy. You may create rapport and trust with people by participating in conversations with them in an authentic manner and demonstrating an interest in the events and viewpoints of others. Additionally, having an awareness of nonverbal clues, like body language and facial expressions, may assist in the development of a feeling of understanding and connection with the other person.

Adding value to the experiences of others is an additional essential component of connection development and networking. This may be accomplished in a variety of ways, including the exchange of information or resources, the provision of support or encouragement, etc. You may establish a feeling of reciprocity and show your commitment to the connection by continuously contributing something of value to the other party. This kind of two-way communication helps to solidify ties and cultivate long-lasting partnerships.

The practice of following up with contacts is a vital component of networking that is sometimes disregarded despite its significance in preserving ties. Take the time to reach out to someone after meeting someone new or getting back in touch with an old friend in order to convey your gratitude for the opportunity to contact them. This simple action serves to strengthen the connection, and it reveals that you are really interested in maintaining the connection.

It is just as crucial to keep the relationships you already have as it is to make new connections. Maintaining touch with your contacts on a consistent basis, whether it be via a phone call, an email, or a message sent through social media, can allow you to demonstrate that you care about them as well as keep you updated about their lives. Congratulate them on their achievements and be there for them when they face challenges; this will help to develop the connection between you.

Authenticity is an essential component for the development of fruitful interpersonal connections. Deeper ties and trust may be fostered when people are authentic in their interactions with one another, demonstrate vulnerability, and share their actual selves. When people have a positive impression of another person's integrity and authenticity, they are more willing to invest in connection with that person. Embracing honesty lays the groundwork for developing meaningful and long-lasting interactions with other people.

The role of networking in building success and wealth

In today's linked society, one of the most important factors in determining one's level of success and riches is networking. It entails forming connections with people who can give you resources, expertise, and opportunities that contribute to your personal and professional development and then maintaining those relationships over time. In this in-depth study, we will examine the importance of networking in terms of gaining success and amassing riches by focusing on eight fundamental facets of the topic.

Accessing Opportunities and Resources

The access to opportunities and resources that may be gained by networking is one of the key advantages of doing so. You may open doors to possible career vacancies, collaboration chances, and investment prospects if you create contacts with people working in a variety of different businesses and roles. These relationships may also give you significant resources, such as insights into the sector, introductions to key persons, and access to specialist expertise, all of which can help your success and the creation of wealth.

Expanding Your Skill Set and Knowledge Base

Building your knowledge and skill base may be significantly aided by growing your network of professional contacts. You will have the opportunity to be exposed to new ideas, methods, and points of view if you engage in conversation with professionals whose backgrounds and fields of expertise are broad. This broader knowledge may help boost your problem-solving talents, creativity, and flexibility, all of which are critical characteristics for attaining success in today's fast-changing world and accumulating wealth.

Building Credibility and Reputation

Building your credibility and reputation in the industry that you've chosen might be facilitated by a robust network. You may show that you are dedicated to high standards of quality and excellence by associating yourself with reputable persons and organizations. Your network may also be able to vouch for your talents, work ethic, and character, which will increase your reputation in the eyes of prospective employers, business partners, and investors. Because it encourages faith and confidence in one's capabilities, having a good reputation is one of the most important factors in obtaining success and amassing money.

Facilitating Collaboration and Partnerships

Networking is an extremely important activity that plays an important part in fostering cooperation and partnerships, both of which may help your success and your attempts to develop wealth. You may open the door to chances for partnerships that are advantageous to both parties by cultivating relationships with organizations and people who share your values. These collaborations may help you broaden your reach, combine resources and experience, and capitalize on the qualities of each party involved, which can speed up your progress toward achieving your objectives.

Providing Mentorship and Support

Building a successful career and amassing financial security are two goals that need access to guidance and assistance at various points along the way. Mentors with years of experience may provide insightful direction, sound counsel, and positive reinforcement, which can assist you in overcoming obstacles and making more educated choices. This assistance may have a big influence on both your personal and professional development by providing you with insights and viewpoints that can help speed your journey toward success and the acquisition of wealth.

Enhancing Personal Growth and Self-awareness

Networking may help you develop personally and become more self-aware, both of which are essential for obtaining success and accumulating riches. You may obtain a more in-depth awareness of your own strengths and shortcomings, as well as opportunities for improvement, by interacting with others whose lives have been shaped by a wide range of experiences and backgrounds. Because of this self-awareness, you are able to work on your own personal growth, improve your strategy, and ultimately boost your odds of being successful in anything you set out to do.

Encouraging Accountability and Motivation

In your quest for success and money, a strong network may also inspire responsibility and serve as a source of encouragement for you. Your connections may help you develop a feeling of responsibility, which will motivate you to take regular action and advance toward your objectives when you share your goals and dreams with them. In addition, seeing the achievements of other people in your network may serve as a source of motivation and inspiration, propelling you to go on and accomplish the things you have set out to do.

Expanding Your Sphere of Influence

Your sphere of influence is an essential component in gaining success and accumulating riches, and networking is a great way to considerably extend it. Your capacity to interact with a more diverse audience, communicate your ideas, and influence those who make decisions will increase in tandem with the size of your network. This increased visibility and influence may lead to new opportunities, collaborations, and investments, all of which can add to your total success and wealth accumulation if you take advantage of them.

Tips for effective networking and relationship building

Building strong relationships and engaging in effective networking are essential skills that may open doors to a vast array of possibilities and resources in both your personal and professional lives. You may lay a solid foundation for your future success and money growth if you acquire and perfect these talents. This book will discuss six fundamental principles for successful networking and connection development, presenting insights that can be put into action to improve your ability to network.

Cultivate a Genuine Interest in Others

Developing a genuine interest in the people you are networking with is one of the essential components of successful networking. Those who demonstrate a real interest in other people and compassion have a natural ability to attract others. When participating in discussions, it is important to provide questions with open-ended answers and to pay attention to the replies. When you do so, you exhibit your willingness to understand the viewpoints and experiences of others, which fosters trust and rapport between you and those other individuals. This kind of real curiosity will provide the groundwork for solid, long-lasting friendships that may significantly contribute to your achievement.

Develop Your Communication Skills

When it comes to developing successful relationships and networks, effective communication is very necessary. Place your primary emphasis on developing your active listening, public speaking, and nonverbal communication abilities. When you are listening to other people, it is important to communicate that you are engaged by maintaining eye contact, nodding in agreement, and providing vocal comments. When you talk, make sure that your opinions are articulated in a way that is clear and succinct and that you use narrative tactics to make your ideas more interesting. In addition, be conscious of your body language and facial expressions, and make it a point to ensure that they reflect an open and receptive attitude. You will be able to forge meaningful relationships, which are the bedrock of professional development and accomplishment if you work on improving your communication abilities.

Be Proactive and Strategic

Approaching networking with proactivity and strategy is required for it to be successful. Establish concrete networking objectives, such as the establishment of a certain number of new connections or the participation in a certain amount of events on a monthly basis. Do some research into the industry events, conferences, and online forums that are relevant to your area of work and provide opportunities to network with other experts. Find people within your current network who can either put you in touch with new connections or provide you with insightful advice, and do both of these things. You may optimize the chances available to you for developing meaningful contacts if you approach your networking endeavors with a proactive and purposeful mindset.

Offer Value and Support

Providing value and assistance to your contacts is one of the most efficient ways to develop great relationships, and it's also one of the most rewarding. This may be accomplished in a variety of ways, including the exchange of expertise, the provision of introductions, or the offer of aid with a project. You may show your dedication to the connection and establish a feeling of reciprocity by delivering value on a constant basis. This will motivate people to support you in return and will build a sense of reciprocity. The giving and receiving of benefits by both parties help to solidify connections and cultivate long-term relationships, both of which are important for achieving success.

Maintain and Nurture Connections

It is not enough to just make new connections in order for networking to be effective; it is also necessary to nurture and care for the connections that have already been made. Maintain consistent contact with your relationships, keeping them informed of your advancements and demonstrating genuine interest in their life. Honor their achievements and provide assistance and comfort when they are going through difficult circumstances. In addition, you should make an attempt to revive inactive connections since these individuals could give helpful resources or ideas if you can get in touch with them again. You may build a strong network that will help both your personal and professional development if you focus on preserving and cultivating the ties you already have.

Embrace Authenticity and Vulnerability

Embrace genuineness and a willingness to be vulnerable in the course of your networking and relationship-building endeavours. Those who are authentic, honest, and open about their experiences and feelings are more likely to form meaningful connections with other people. Discuss your interests, difficulties, and personal experiences with others to open up the potential for more meaningful interactions. Because of your genuineness and willingness to put yourself out there, you will stand out from the crowd and cultivate trust and rapport, both of which are necessary components of long-lasting partnerships.

The benefits of having a strong support network

In both your personal and professional life, having a solid network of people you can rely on is an extremely significant tool. It gives you access to a wealth of tools, information, and encouragement, all of which may have a big influence on your overall performance and quality of life. We will go over each and every one of the various advantages that come along with having a strong support network in just a moment.

In the first place, having a strong support network during difficult times is beneficial for receiving emotional assistance. Your capacity to deal with anxiety and strain is directly correlated to how well you have a support system in place, and having a network of people on whom you can depend in challenging times may make a huge difference in this regard. When you are going through a difficult circumstance, having people in your support network who are there to lend an ear, give you advice, or just be there when you need someone to depend on may help you handle the issue with more resilience and calm.

Second, having a solid support system around you may be an invaluable source of assistance and mentoring. It doesn't matter whether you're switching careers, launching a new company, or tackling a personal obstacle; having knowledgeable people on your side can provide you with vital insights and assistance at each stage of the process. The information and experience that these mentors possess may be passed on to you, allowing you to make better choices and steer clear of any traps. Your support network is able to provide you with direction and mentoring, which may help expedite your personal development and contribute to your accomplishments in general.

Access to resources and opportunities is another advantage that comes with having a robust support network. Your connections may be able to make new contacts, employment vacancies, or prospective collaboration opportunities available to you that are congruent with your aims and ambitions. They may also provide you access to specific expertise, tools, or resources that you otherwise would not have easy access to if you did not have their assistance. This access to resources and opportunities may open doors for you, expand your horizons, and make it easier for you to reach the objectives you have set for yourself.

Your personal development and increased understanding of yourself may both benefit from having a strong support network. You may obtain a more in-depth awareness of your own talents, flaws, and opportunities for improvement by surrounding yourself with a broad group of people who are willing to offer their experiences, viewpoints, and expertise. This increased self-awareness makes it possible for you to seek personal growth and modify your approach, thus improving the likelihood that you will be successful in your personal and professional efforts.

Having a solid support network helps cultivate a feeling of responsibility as well as the drive to achieve one's goals. You will develop a feeling of responsibility and be more likely to take continuous action toward reaching your goals if you talk to the people in your network about the objectives and objectives you have for the future. In addition, seeing the achievements of people in your network may serve as a source of motivation and inspiration, propelling you to go on and follow your goals. This can be a very powerful way to realize your potential.

In addition, having a strong support system may be beneficial to both your mental health and overall well-being. Having meaningful social ties is critical to our mental health because they give us a feeling that we belong somewhere and that we are protected. Regular connection with members of your support network may be an effective way to counteract feelings of isolation, loneliness, and stress, all of which can contribute to a more upbeat attitude and better mental health overall.

Finally, having a solid support network may help you become better at finding solutions to problems and making decisions. You will be able to draw into the collective knowledge and experiences of a varied group of people if you are able to access that group. This will allow you to solve difficulties and make choices based on accurate information. The use of a collaborative approach to problem-solving has the potential to result in creative solutions and enhanced results.

Chapter 7

Investing in Yourself and Your Future

One of the most beneficial and satisfying things you can do for yourself is to make an investment in both your present and your future. You may build a firm foundation for success and happiness in all facets of your life by devoting time, effort, and resources to your own personal growth and development. Putting effort into bettering oneself in any number of areas and by any number of methods may result in considerable gains over the course of time.

Education and further education are two of the most important components of making an investment in oneself. Growing your expertise and body of knowledge on a consistent basis may have a significant impact on your development as a person and as a professional. To maintain a competitive edge in today's environment and to be able to respond effectively to emerging threats and opportunities, it is necessary to engage in continuous learning. This may be participating in seminars or workshops, going to conferences, reading books, or listening to podcasts on subjects that are of interest to you or that are in line with the objectives you have set for yourself. Putting an emphasis on education and learning allows you to make an investment in your intellectual capital while also exposing you to a wider range of opportunities.

Personal growth is yet another essential element of the process of investing in oneself. Developing emotional intelligence and a growth mindset are both essential components of this process, as are the establishment and pursuit of meaningful objectives. Enhancing one's self-awareness, self-confidence, and resiliency via personal growth may be accomplished, and all three of these characteristics are necessary for achieving success and finding happiness. Journaling, meditating, or working with a professional coach are all activities that may help you get useful insights into your own strengths, flaws, and potential development areas.

The maintenance and improvement of one's physical health are equally important investments in both oneself and one's future. A healthy lifestyle should include engaging in consistent physical activity, maintaining nutritious food, and getting an adequate amount of sleep. If you make caring for your physical health a priority, you'll boost not only your general health but also your mental and emotional well-being as a result. You can guarantee that you have the energy, stamina, and mental clarity required to accomplish your objectives and dreams by making an investment in your physical health.

When it comes to investing in yourself, maintaining both your mental and emotional health is essential. It is possible to have a major influence on your overall happiness and level of life satisfaction by cultivating strong connections, practicing mindfulness, and developing healthy coping mechanisms for dealing with stress. Seeking out psychotherapy or counselling, practicing relaxation methods, or participating in support groups are all excellent ways to acquire helpful skills and resources that may assist you in preserving your mental and emotional health.

Investing in yourself and your future requires that you have a solid understanding of personal finance and do some preparation. Having a solid grasp of personal finance, as well as how to create a budget and make investments, may assist you in making educated choices about your own financial well-being. You can take charge of your future and establish the basis for financial independence and stability by developing a financial plan and setting long-term financial objectives for yourself. You may get access to resources, information, and opportunities that can contribute to your success by cultivating relationships with persons who have similar values and perspectives as you. Additionally, networking may give you emotional support, mentoring, and direction, all of which are very useful assets in both your personal and professional lives.

The importance of self-investment in personal development

A person's personal development is an ongoing process that includes self-improvement, progress, and the discovery of oneself throughout their whole life. You may build a solid foundation for success, happiness, and contentment in all facets of your life by investing in yourself. This will allow you to make the most of your life. This all-encompassing book will examine the significance of self-investment in terms of personal growth. It will focus on five main areas, each of which is one in which investing in oneself may result in considerable long-term rewards.

Enhancing Knowledge and Skills

Continuously expanding your knowledge and capabilities is an essential component of self-investment in personal growth, and it is one of the most important factors to focus on. Continuous education is necessary in today's fast-evolving environment in order to maintain a competitive edge and be able to respond effectively to emerging threats and opportunities. Increasing your knowledge and skill set may provide you access to previously inaccessible opportunities, give you a confidence boost, and make you more marketable to potential employers.

You may increase the value of your intellectual capital by devoting time, energy, and resources to furthering your education and learning. This may be participating in seminars or workshops, going to conferences, reading books, or listening to podcasts on subjects that are of interest to you or that are in line with the objectives you have set for yourself. You may provide a strong foundation for both your personal development and your professional accomplishments by making education and learning a top priority.

Fostering Emotional Intelligence and Mental Health

Personal growth depends heavily on one's emotional quotient as well as their mental state of well-being. The capacity to detect, comprehend, and successfully control one's own emotions, as well as those of others, is what is meant by the term "emotional intelligence." It is an essential element in efficient communication, the development of relationships, and the process of making decisions.

Putting effort into developing your emotional intelligence may result in enhanced self-awareness, empathy, and resiliency—all of which are crucial characteristics for both individual and professional achievement. You may get useful insights into your emotional landscape and be equipped with skills to efficiently navigate your emotions by engaging in activities such as writing, meditating, or obtaining professional counseling. These activities can help you navigate your emotions more effectively.

When it comes to investing in yourself, giving priority to your mental health is just as vital. It is possible to have a major influence on your overall happiness and level of life satisfaction by cultivating strong connections, practicing mindfulness, and developing healthy coping mechanisms for dealing with stress. When you put effort into improving your mental health, you lay the groundwork for your own future growth and development as a person.

Cultivating a Growth Mindset and Goal Setting

A growth mindset is a view that one's talents, intellect, and skills can be developed and improved through the application of work and devotion, as opposed to a fixed mentality, which is the opinion that one's abilities, intelligence, and skills cannot be developed or improved. The cultivation of a growth mindset is an essential component of self-investment in personal development because it helps you to accept difficulties, gain insight from mistakes, and remain resolute in the face of adversity.

You may expedite your own personal development and broaden your horizons by cultivating a growth mindset, and so opening yourself up to new opportunities and experiences. A growth mindset may be developed in conjunction with other strategies, such as setting and working toward meaningful objectives. The process of defining goals may offer you direction, inspiration, and a sense of purpose, so directing your path toward personal growth and assisting you in monitoring your advancement along the way.

Building a Strong Support Network

Along the path of your personal growth, having a solid support network is a very useful commodity. You may foster development and progress in yourself by cultivating an atmosphere that is favorable to it by surrounding yourself with people who think and act similarly to you and who share your ideals, objectives, and objectives.

Putting effort into developing and maintaining healthy connections with people in your life, such as friends, family, mentors, and coworkers, may give you access to emotional support, advice, resources, and opportunities that can help your own personal development. You will be able to make choices that are more informed, as well as overcome problems and speed up your growth if you use the aggregate expertise and experiences of your support network.

Pursuing Passions and Hobbies

Putting time and effort into your interests and hobbies is an essential component of personal growth and development. Taking part in pursuits that provide you with pleasure and contentment may help you feel less stressed, can stimulate your creativity, and can give you a sense of purpose. You are making an investment in your general well-being and happiness, which will eventually promote your personal development when you commit time and resources to pursue your hobbies.

Strategies for investing in education, health, and personal growth

For a life that is successful and satisfying, it is necessary to make investments in one's education, health, and personal development. You may build a solid foundation for both your personal and professional success by devoting time, effort, and resources to the aforementioned areas. This thorough book will highlight six important areas where you can have a big influence on your overall well-being and development, sharing techniques for investing in education, health, and personal growth. These are the areas where you can make a substantial impact on your overall well-being and development.

Embracing Lifelong Learning

Continuing your education throughout your life is one of the most important components of making an investment in your education. It is vital to continually increase your knowledge and abilities in order to stay competitive and flexible in the modern world, which is a world that is evolving at a fast rate. This may be participating in seminars or workshops, going to conferences, reading books, or listening to podcasts on subjects that are of interest to you or that are in line with the objectives you have set for yourself.

Create a learning plan that specifies your educational objectives and the resources you will utilize to attain them in order to embrace learning as a process that continues throughout your life. Set aside time, maybe once a day or once a week, to concentrate on your education and monitor your development over time. Putting an emphasis on education and learning allows you to make an investment in your intellectual capital and provide a strong groundwork for both personal development and professional achievement.

Prioritizing Physical Health and Wellness

The maintenance and improvement of one's physical health are essential investments in both oneself and one's future. A healthy lifestyle should include engaging in consistent physical activity, maintaining nutritious food, and getting an adequate amount of sleep. When you make your own physical well-being a top priority, you guarantee that you will have the energy, stamina, and mental clarity necessary to achieve the objectives and dreams that are important to you.

Create a fitness plan that includes a range of activities, such as aerobic exercise, strength training, and flexibility exercises, in order to put your physical health at the forefront of your priorities. You may improve the health of your diet by opting for whole foods, lean meats, and a diet rich in fruits and vegetables. Make healthy food choices. Last but not least, create a consistent routine for your sleeping habits to guarantee that you receive enough rest and recuperation each night.

Focusing on Mental and Emotional Well-being

The maintenance of one's mental and emotional health is crucial to one's overall growth and development as a person. It is possible to have a major influence on your overall happiness and level of life satisfaction by cultivating strong connections, practicing mindfulness, and developing healthy coping mechanisms for dealing with stress.

Consider participating in any kind of relaxation activity, such as yoga, meditation, or deep breathing exercises, so that you may make an investment in your mental and emotional health. You may also want to think about seeing a therapist or counselor in order to address any underlying issues related to your mental health or the difficulties you are having emotionally. Spending time with loved ones and developing a solid support network should also be high on your list of priorities in order to guarantee that you will always have access to emotional support and encouragement when you need it.

Setting Meaningful Goals and Tracking Progress

The achievement of one's goals is an essential component of one's personal growth and development. You may give yourself a feeling of purpose, direction, and drive if you create significant objectives for yourself and work toward achieving those goals. To make the most of the time you spend on goal planning for your own personal development, write down both your long-term and short-term objectives, devise a strategy to accomplish each of those objectives, and check in on your progress on a consistent basis.

When it comes to goal-setting, it's a good idea to think about using the SMART (Specific, Measurable, Achievable, Relevant, and Time-bound) criteria, as this may help guarantee that your objectives are well-defined, achievable, and relevant. Maintaining your motivation and holding yourself responsible for your objectives may be accomplished by regularly evaluating those goals and measuring your progress, which will eventually speed up your personal growth and development.

Developing a Growth Mindset

The concept that one's capabilities, intellect, and skills can be enhanced and improved through the application of work and devotion is referred to as a "growth mindset." It is crucial for personal growth and development to cultivate a growth mindset because it helps you to accept difficulties, learn from failure, and endure in the face of adversity.

In order to cultivate a growth mindset, it is important to place emphasis not only on the consequences of learning but also on the process of learning itself. Accept difficulties as chances for personal development and look at setbacks as instructive possibilities to improve in the future.

The long-term benefits of investing in yourself

Putting money into yourself is one of the wisest and most gratifying decisions you can make for yourself and your future. You may build a firm foundation for success and happiness in all facets of your life by devoting time, effort, and resources to your own personal growth and development. This all-encompassing book will discuss the long-term advantages of investing in yourself and will highlight five important areas in which self-investment may lead to large long-term profits.

Enhanced Knowledge and Skills

Continuously expanding one's knowledge and skill set is a crucial component of the practice of investing in one's own well-being, which is one of the most important parts of this practice. Continuous education is necessary in today's fast-evolving environment in order to maintain a competitive edge and be able to respond effectively to emerging threats and opportunities. Increasing your knowledge and skill set may provide you access to previously inaccessible opportunities, give you a confidence boost, and make you more marketable to potential employers.

You may increase the value of your intellectual capital by devoting time, energy, and resources to furthering your education and learning. This investment may result in a range of long-term rewards, including greater earning potential, job progression, and the capacity to explore new and exciting activities in both your personal and professional lives.

Improved Mental and Emotional Well-being

It is essential, for both short-term and long-term success and enjoyment, to make an investment in one's mental and emotional well-being. It is possible to have a major influence on your overall happiness and level of life satisfaction by cultivating strong connections, practicing mindfulness, and developing healthy coping mechanisms for dealing with stress.

You may build a strong basis for your own personal growth and development by putting effort into maintaining your mental and emotional health. This investment may result in long-term advantages such as enhanced resiliency and emotional intelligence, as well as the capability to overcome obstacles and disappointments with greater ease. Enhanced mental and emotional health may also have a beneficial effect on your relationships, profession, and the general level of joy you get from life.

Stronger Personal and Professional Relationships

When you invest in yourself, one of the most important things you can do is cultivate and grow your personal and professional connections. You may foster development and progress in yourself by cultivating an atmosphere that is favorable to it by surrounding yourself with people who think and act similarly to you and who share your ideals, objectives, and objectives.

Building and sustaining connections is an investment that may pay off in the long run with advantages such as emotional support, direction, and access to resources and opportunities that can contribute to one's own personal development. You may overcome obstacles, make better choices, and speed up your personal growth with the assistance of a solid support network, all of which can eventually lead to a life that is more successful and meaningful for you.

Increased Financial Security and Independence

When you invest in yourself, and your future, one of the most important things you can do is work on improving your financial knowledge and planning skills. Having a solid grasp of personal finance, as well as how to create a budget and make investments, may assist you in making educated choices about your own financial well-being. You can take charge of your future and establish the basis for financial independence and stability by developing a financial plan and setting long-term financial objectives for yourself.

Investing in your financial knowledge and preparation may have long-term advantages, such as lowering the amount of financial stress you experience, increasing the amount of money you save, and giving you the capacity to become financially independent. This investment not only improves your current circumstances but also provides the basis for a bright and wealthy future. It ensures that you are well-equipped to negotiate the financial problems that you will face throughout your life and to grasp opportunities that will come your way.

Greater Fulfillment and Life Satisfaction

Spending time and money on your interests, activities, and growth as an individual may help you live a life that is more satisfying and well-rounded. Taking part in pursuits that provide you with pleasure and contentment may help you feel less stressed, can stimulate your creativity, and can give you a sense of purpose. You are making an investment in your general well-being and happiness when you devote time and resources to pursuing your hobbies.

Investing in your own personal development, interests, and hobbies may have long-term rewards such as enhanced life satisfaction, a feeling of purpose, and a life that is more balanced and well-rounded. You may build a solid foundation for your own personal satisfaction and happiness, which will eventually lead to a more successful and rewarding life, provided you make an investment in yourself.

Chapter 8

Wealth Building Strategies

The accumulation of wealth is a necessary step toward obtaining monetary autonomy and assuring a prosperous future for oneself and one's loved ones, and it is one of the most important goals that one may pursue. You may achieve a consistent increase in your wealth over time by engaging in a variety of financial tactics and buying a wide range of assets.

Beginning to save money as soon as possible is one of the most important steps in the process of accumulating wealth. If you start putting money away for your future sooner rather than later, you will give the power of compound interest more time to work for you. If you make it a regular practice to save aside some of the money you earn each month, you will be well on your way to amassing financial security.

A well-planned budget will assist you in better managing your spending, identifying areas in which you can make cost reductions, and ensuring that you have the funds to invest in opportunities that will help you develop wealth. You may get control of your financial situation and create the road for long-term financial success by developing a budget for your household and sticking to it.

When it comes to accumulating money, you should make paying off debts with high-interest rates a top priority. Because a considerable amount of your income goes toward paying interest on high-interest debt, this may considerably limit your capacity to save money and invest it in the future. Your priority should be to pay off high-interest debt as fast as you can so that you have more money available for investments in your future.

Increasing one's wealth is accomplished in large part via the practice of investing in a variety of assets. Having a diversified investment portfolio that includes stocks, bonds, real estate, and other assets may assist in lowering overall risk while simultaneously increasing potential profits over time. Learn as much as you can about the many investment opportunities available, and consult with experts in the field to help you construct a diversified investment portfolio that is appropriate for your level of comfort with taking on risk.

Increasing the amount of money you might potentially earn is another critical component of accumulating wealth. Always be on the lookout for opportunities to improve your financial situation, such as seeking promotions, advancing your schooling or obtaining certificates, or engaging in additional work on the side. You will be able to save and invest more money, which will speed up the process of creating wealth if you increase your income.

It is essential to do routine reviews and make necessary adjustments to your financial plan in order to ensure that you remain on track to achieve your objectives regarding the accumulation of wealth. Your financial condition, the objectives you want to achieve, and the priorities you have should all be reflected in your financial plan. You should do regular checks to verify that your strategy is in line with your current requirements and goals, and you should make any required changes to ensure that your efforts to grow wealth remain on track.

The establishment of an emergency fund is a crucial component in the process of amassing wealth since it serves as a financial buffer in the event of unforeseen expenditures or a reduction in income. If you have an emergency fund, you won't have to delve into your assets or depend on high-interest loans to meet unanticipated costs, which will eventually help safeguard your wealth.

It may be beneficial to seek the guidance of those who have experience in the financial industry while you work to develop your wealth. You may benefit from the useful insights, recommendations, and assistance in decision-making that financial counsellors, planners, and investment specialists can give you with regard to your future financial situation. You may optimize your efforts to generate wealth and increase your prospects of long-term financial success by harnessing the experience of financial experts. This will allow you to maximize both of these potential outcomes.

Key wealth-building strategies and principles

Increasing one's money is a process that may take a lifetime and calls for unwavering commitment and self-control, in addition to a solid comprehension of a variety of financial techniques and fundamentals. You may build a solid foundation for long-term financial success by using a mix of strategies that have been shown to be effective and by adopting the appropriate mentality. You will be able to establish a firm grasp of the fundamental aspects of amassing money with the assistance of this thorough book, which will present vital wealth-building tactics and ideas.

The Importance of Saving and Budgeting

Creating a solid saving and budgeting habit is one of the essential elements that contribute to the process of generating wealth. The act of laying away a part of one's salary for use at a later time is referred to as saving, while budgeting refers to the process of allocating one's income to a variety of costs and financial objectives. You may regain control of your financial situation, cut costs that aren't required, and guarantee that you have enough money to invest in chances that will help you grow wealth if you save money on a regular basis and stick to a budget that you've carefully laid out.

Create a comprehensive budget that includes your monthly income and costs as a first step toward building a solid habit of saving money and sticking to a spending plan. Set aside a certain amount of money each month for savings, with the goal of putting away at least 10–20 percent of your monthly earnings. Maintain a close eye on your spending habits and be willing to make necessary changes to your spending plan and financial plan in order to guarantee that you are constantly able to reach your savings and financial objectives.

Diversifying Investments for Long-Term Growth

When it comes to amassing money, diversification is one of the most important principles to adhere to since it helps to decrease risk and maximize returns over time. You may lower your overall risk exposure and increase your potential returns by diversifying your holdings across a number of asset classes, such as stocks, bonds, real estate, and other investment vehicles. This allows you to capitalize on the expansionary potential of a wide range of markets and businesses.

To start building a varied investment portfolio, you should first educate yourself about the many investment opportunities available and then seek assistance from specialists in the financial industry. When deciding which investments to include in your portfolio, it is important to take into account your long-term investing horizon, your level of comfort with risk, and your financial objectives. You should do routine checks and rebalancing on your investment portfolio to ensure that it continues to be well-diversified and in line with your long-term financial goals.

Maximizing Income Potential through Career Advancement and Side Hustles

Growing your income is one of the most important steps in the process of accumulating wealth because it paves the way for you to put away and spend more money over time. You may increase your earning potential and accelerate your attempts to acquire wealth by engaging in a number of different techniques, including pursuing job development, furthering your education, obtaining professional certifications, and engaging in side hustles.

Conduct frequent self-evaluations of your professional development and be on the lookout for new learning and advancement possibilities to optimize your earning potential. Increasing your worth on the job market and improving your career chances both require that you make investments in your education and professional abilities. In addition, give some thought to the possibility of engaging in some freelancing or part-time employment on the side in order to increase the rate at which you amass riches.

Adopting a Long-Term Mindset and Financial Discipline

The accumulation of wealth is a process that takes place over a lengthy period of time and calls for patience, perseverance, and financial discipline. Adopting a long-term perspective requires you to keep your attention fixed on the objectives you want to achieve with your finances and to make decisions that are in line with those goals on a continuous basis, despite the presence of short-term temptations or obstacles.

Maintaining a continuous practice of saving money, keeping to your budget, and making educated judgments about your investments are all aspects of practicing financial discipline. You will be able to remain focused on your objectives for developing money and progressively gain wealth over time if you cultivate financial discipline and a mentality that is oriented toward the long term.

Leveraging the Power of Compound Interest

The notion of compound interest is an effective tool for accumulating money and may considerably quicken the pace at which your wealth increases. When you earn interest on an investment and then reinvest that money, this is called compound interest because it enables you to earn interest not only on the initial investment but also on the interest that has been collected. This impact may, over time, lead to exponential growth in your assets, significantly increasing the likelihood that you will amass a substantial amount of money.

To get the most out of the potential benefits of compound interest, you need to begin saving at an early age and maintain that investment throughout time. The longer your assets have to accumulate interest and dividends, the greater the potential for a substantial increase.

Various investment opportunities

Investing is an essential part of the process of amassing money since it enables you to expand your wealth and produce passive income over the course of time. You will be in a better position to establish a diverse investment portfolio that is suited to your financial objectives and level of risk tolerance if you have a solid grasp of the numerous investment choices available, such as stocks, real estate, and business ownership. You will get a firm grasp of each investment opportunity and the possible rewards associated with it with the aid of this comprehensive guide, which will cover these options in depth.

Stocks - Owning a Piece of a Company

When you invest in stocks, you buy shares of a company, which gives you a stake in that firm and makes you a partial owner of it. As a shareholder, you have the opportunity to benefit from the expansion and profitability of the firm, most often via the appreciation of your investment and the receipt of dividend payments. Because stocks have traditionally generated very high returns over relatively long time periods, purchasing them might be seen as an appealing investment choice for the purpose of wealth creation.

You may purchase individual shares of a company's stock via a brokerage account, or you can invest in a mutual fund or exchange-traded fund (ETF) that contains a diversified portfolio of companies. Both of these options allow you to engage in the stock market. When it comes to constructing a successful stock portfolio, some of the most important tasks are doing research on businesses, gaining a grasp of market patterns, and determining how much risk you are willing to take. Reviewing and readjusting the weighting of your stock holdings on a regular basis may assist in ensuring that your investment portfolio continues to reflect your desired long-term financial outcomes.

Real Estate - Investing in Tangible Assets

Investing in real estate is the purchase of tangible assets, such as residential or commercial buildings, with the intention of earning money via rental payments or making a profit when the property is sold. Because of the consistent stream of passive income, they may give, the potential for capital gain, and the tax advantages they can bring, real estate investments are an appealing choice for the creation of wealth.

Investing in real estate may be done in a variety of ways, such as via direct property ownership, real estate investment trusts (REITs), or crowd funding platforms that specialize in real estate. When selecting a real estate investment strategy, it is vital to carefully analyze your financial objectives, level of comfort with risk, and investing preferences. Since each technique provides varying degrees of risk, engagement, and possible returns, the decision must be made after thorough consideration of these factors.

Business Ownership - Becoming an Entrepreneur

One of the most satisfying and possibly profitable investment opportunities is the ownership of a company. You have the ability, as a person who owns a company, to establish and cultivate a prosperous enterprise, which may result in the production of money via the running of the business, as well as the possibility of selling the firm in the future for a profit. The ownership of a business calls for commitment, tenacity of effort, and entrepreneurial abilities, but it also has the ability to significantly increase one's wealth.

One may acquire ownership of a company via a variety of means, including the purchase of an already established company, the launch of one's own company from scratch, or the purchase of a franchise. Before deciding to become a company owner, it is essential to do a thorough analysis of your abilities, areas of interest, and available resources in order to properly prepare for the many obstacles, dangers, and possible rewards that are associated with the various options.

Bonds - Lending Money to Governments or Corporations

When you invest in bonds, you are essentially lending money to governments or businesses, with the expectation that you will be repaid with interest after a certain amount of time. It's common knowledge that bonds have a lower level of risk than stocks do, and they also have the potential to provide a consistent flow of income in the form of interest payments. They may be a crucial part of a diverse investment portfolio, bringing both stability and the possibility of income. Therefore it is important to include them.

You may either invest in bond mutual funds or exchange-traded funds (ETFs), or you can buy bonds directly via your brokerage account. If you want to make sure that your bond investments are in line with your financial objectives and the amount of risk you are willing to take, it is essential to take into account the credit quality of the bond, the risk of fluctuating interest rates, and the term of the bond.

Peer-to-Peer Lending - Investing in Personal or Business Loans

Investing in personal or company loans that are granted via online platforms that link borrowers and investors is an example of peer-to-peer lending, often known as P2P lending. Because you are able to invest in a range of loans that all have various interest rates and degrees of risk, peer-to-peer lending may provide you with excellent returns as well as the advantages of diversification.

When engaging in peer-to-peer lending, it is very necessary to thoroughly evaluate the reliability of the platform, the loan underwriting rules, and the diversification choices. You may mitigate risk and possibly make great returns from your peer-to-peer lending investments if you distribute your investments over numerous loans and pick borrowers with solid credit histories with care.

Alternative Investments - Exploring Unconventional Options

Alternative investments include a broad spectrum of non-traditional asset classes, including private equity, commodities, and collectibles, amongst others. These investments often come with heightened risks and may need specific knowledge or skill. However, they might potentially provide advantages related to diversification as well as the possibility of large profits.

Examples of alternative investments include precious metals (such as gold and silver), art and collectibles, crypto currencies, and investments in private enterprises or startups. Other examples of alternative investments include real estate and collectibles. When contemplating alternative investment possibilities, it is essential to do exhaustive research on the particular asset in question and have a solid understanding of the risks involved. Compared to standard investment choices, alternative investments are often more volatile and subject to fewer regulations.

Tips for managing and growing personal wealth

Budgeting and saving:

Making a budget and adhering to it should be considered one of the most important aspects of managing one's own finances. Having a budget enables you to keep track of both your income and your costs, as well as to establish savings and spending targets. To begin developing a budget, you should first determine your regular monthly income and expenditures, including those for rent or mortgage, utilities, and transportation costs. The next step is to keep track of your variable spending, such as food, entertainment, and eating out. When you have a crystal clear picture of where your money is going, you can begin to pinpoint areas in which you may reduce your expenditure and so increase the amount of money you save. This might involve bringing lunch from home rather than dining out, canceling subscriptions that are not being utilized, or cutting down on the expense of transportation by carpooling or utilizing public transit. Make sure that your objectives for saving money are attainable, and think about employing technologies that can help you save money automatically so that the process is less difficult. This may include utilizing applications that round up your purchases and deposit the difference into a savings account, or it could involve setting up automatic payments to a savings account.

Investing:

Investing is one of the most productive strategies to increase your own wealth over the course of a longer period of time. There is a wide range of investment opportunities available to people today, some of which include real estate, stocks, bonds, and mutual funds. The trick is to identify the correct combination of assets that fit in with your financial objectives and the amount of risk you are willing to take.

Learn as much as you can about the various investment alternatives and methods before you make any investments. Think about getting the assistance of a financial adviser who can guide you in the creation of an investment strategy that is tailored to your requirements. Be careful to diversify your holdings in order to cut your risk, and keep a close eye on your portfolio on a consistent basis to ensure it continues to perform as expected. It is crucial to keep in mind that investing entails risk and that there is no assurance of profits. Because of this, it is critical to approach it with a long-term perspective and to avoid making rash choices based on short-term shifts in the market.

Managing debt:

Debt can be such a significant roadblock to the accumulation of personal wealth, it is critical to ensure that it is well managed. You should begin by making a list of all of your bills, which should include things like credit cards, loans, and mortgages, and developing a strategy to pay them off as soon as you possibly can. Think about paying off the loan with the highest interest rate first and making additional payments whenever you can. It could be beneficial to investigate the possibility of consolidating your debts or refinancing your loans in order to get lower interest rates. Make it a priority to avoid taking on any more debt unless doing so is really required and can be accommodated within your financial plan. If you are having trouble keeping up with your financial obligations, you may want to consider getting assistance from a credit counseling organization or a financial counselor who can assist you in formulating a strategy to get your finances back on track.

Chapter 9

The Journey to Lasting Change

It is a process that demands effort, patience, and a desire to take regular action over time in order to bring about changes that are long-lasting. To bring about transformations that are long-lasting, it is necessary to devise objectives that are distinct, quantifiable, attainable, pertinent, and time-bound. Putting your objectives in writing and making a habit of reviewing them on a regular basis will help you stay motivated and focused. It is essential that you divide your objectives into manageable subtasks that may be carried out on a daily or weekly basis if you want to achieve them.

It is really necessary to design a strategy in order to realize your objectives. This strategy may involve the creation of a timetable, the establishment of deadlines, and the identification of certain activities that you need to perform in order to come closer to achieving your objectives. You can maintain your motivation and keep on track with your strategy by first breaking it down into more manageable subtasks and then monitoring your progress on a regular basis. If you discover that you are having difficulty moving forward with your plans, you may want to try modifying them in order to make them more attainable, such as by breaking down your objectives into even more granular stages.

To make a change that is long-lasting, constant activity over a period of time is required. It is necessary to establish a committee to work towards your objectives by moving in baby increments each and every day. This might be engaging in thirty minutes of physical activity, committing to a mindfulness practice, or making connections with possible mentors. In spite of the difficulties or failures you may have, it is essential to maintain your motivation and concentration. If you discover that you are having difficulty taking action, you may want to try modifying your plan or looking for guidance from a coach, a mentor, or an accountability partner.

Accountability is a potent weapon that may be used to create changes that are long-lasting. Think about telling other people about your plans and soliciting their help and motivation in reaching your objectives. Participating in a support group, working with a coach, or finding a person to whom you are accountable for your activities by helping you remain on track and holding you responsible for your acts are all helpful options. It is possible to remain on track with your goals by regularly assessing your progress and modifying your strategy in accordance with the requirements of the situation.

Taking care of oneself is one of the most important aspects of bringing about a change that will endure. It is essential to place a high priority on self-care and to take care of both your physical and mental health by, among other things, obtaining an adequate amount of sleep, eating a good diet, working out on a regular basis, and engaging in relaxation practices such as yoga and meditation. You can keep your motivation up and keep your concentration on your objectives by giving yourself breaks when you need them and giving things that offer you pleasure and satisfaction a higher priority.

The acceptance of past mistakes is another crucial component. The process of making changes that are long-lasting often requires struggling through obstacles and falling short along the way. Keep in mind that making mistakes is an inevitable component of the educational process and may serve as a source of really useful knowledge. It is essential to gain insight from past mistakes and make necessary adjustments to one's strategy in order to guarantee that one remains on course.

The importance of embracing change and adapting habits

The Benefits of Embracing Change:

Accepting change as a natural part of life is one of the most important aspects of one's own growth and development. When you show that you are prepared to accept change, you develop the ability to adapt and become more receptive to novel experiences. You also acquire a growth mindset, which enables you to see problems as chances to learn better as a result of your experiences. Embracing change may also assist you in developing a deeper sense of self-awareness as well as a more robust sense of purpose. If you are prepared to accept change, you will develop more self-assurance in your capacity to handle the highs and lows of life and craft a life that is meaningful to you.

Increasing one's resilience is one of the primary advantages that come from being open to change. If you are willing to adjust to new circumstances, you will find that you are better equipped to deal with stress and prevail in the face of adversity. You improve your ability to solve problems and become more creative in the ways that you approach finding answers to issues. Accepting change is one way to bring about growth in one's own self-awareness. You may get a deeper understanding of yourself, as well as your capabilities and limitations, by being open to trying new things and taking calculated risks. This may help you make more informed choices and build a life that brings you greater satisfaction.

Why Habits Matter:

Our everyday lives are built upon the basis of our habits. It refers to the inconspicuous, routine activities that we carry out on a daily basis without giving them a second thought. Our lifestyle choices, whether they be good or bad habits, may have a big influence on the course of our lives. Developing beneficial routines, such as going to the gym on a regular basis or eating a diet rich in fruits and vegetables, may help us feel better and be more productive. Habits that are harmful to one's health, such as smoking or putting things off, might have the reverse impact. We should prioritize developing habits since they enable us to make more efficient use of our mental resources and make it simpler to achieve our objectives. If we develop healthy routines, we may get closer to achieving our objectives without having to depend only on our own willpower to do so.

One of the primary reasons why habits are important is because they may have a substantial influence on the success and enjoyment of our lives over the long run. Our daily routines are shaped by our habits, which in turn determine how we allocate our time and energy. We have the ability to create a life that is more satisfying and fruitful by cultivating beneficial habits. Developing healthy routines may also make it simpler for us to accomplish our objectives by making it less difficult for us to take constant action over the course of time. Why are habits so important? Because they assist us in gradually constructing the life we desire out of a series of little steps.

The Importance of Adapting Habits:

Changing one's routine is one of the most important aspects of personal growth and development. When we are willing to adjust our routines, we become more resistant to the effects of change and more flexible in our responses to it. To modify our routines and behaviors so that they are more in line with our objectives and principles, we need to be ready to adapt our habits. It is necessary for us to maintain an open mind toward new concepts and a willingness to explore a variety of alternative methods. Altering our routines may also assist us in breaking rid of unfavorable patterns and establishing new, more favorable patterns in their stead. When we are willing to make changes to our routines, it helps us become more self-aware and increases our capacity to create the kind of life we desire for ourselves.

Changing our routines in order to bring about long-term improvements in our lives is one of the primary benefits associated with developing new habits. We are able to break away from unproductive patterns and establish new, more productive patterns by making little adjustments to our routines. This has the potential to contribute to improvements in health as well as increases in both happiness and productivity. Changing our habits may also make it easier for us to attain our objectives by making it simpler for us to execute the same actions on a regular basis over time. When we are open to changing our routines, we give ourselves the opportunity to take the baby steps necessary to build the life we see for ourselves.

How Embracing Change and Adapting Habits Can Improve Your Life:

Acceptance of change and the development of new routines may have a considerable influence on the course of one's life. You will become more flexible to different situations and open to new experiences if you embrace change. This may result in enhanced personal development and resilience, as well as new possibilities. Changing your routines may assist you in breaking free of unproductive patterns and establishing new, more productive patterns in their place. This has the potential to contribute to improvements in health as well as increases in both happiness and productivity. These tactics, when combined, have the ability to assist you in realizing your full potential and crafting a life that is more satisfying and meaningful to you.

Increasing one's self-awareness is one of the primary advantages of being open to change and modifying one's routines. You may get a deeper understanding of yourself, as well as your capabilities and limitations, by being open to trying new things and taking calculated risks. This may help you make more informed choices and build a life that brings you greater satisfaction. Accepting change and making adjustments to one's routine may also result in enhanced self-assurance and resiliency. When you are willing to adapt to new conditions and take chances, you become more capable of managing stress and overcoming adversity. When you are ready to adapt to new situations and take risks, this may assist you in achieving your objectives and creating the life you have always imagined for yourself.

Strategies for maintaining momentum and staying on the path to success

Develop a Daily Routine:

Establishing a regular schedule for oneself is an effective tactic for continuing one's forward motion and remaining on the road to achievement. When you follow the same pattern each day, you give your life structure and stability. This is what happens when you have a routine. Even if you run across obstacles or experience a setback, this may help you maintain your concentration and keep up your productivity.

To establish a consistent pattern for each day, you should begin by listing your top priorities and allocating your time appropriately. Make sure to include time in your schedule for critical activities like working out and working, as well as time for you to rest and take care of yourself. You may maintain your drive and concentration on the road to achievement by establishing a daily routine that is congruent with the objectives and ideals you have set for yourself.

It is also essential to have a flexible mindset and adapt your schedule according to the circumstances. Because of the unpredictability of life, there may be moments when you will need to adjust to changes that were not anticipated. You can keep moving forward toward your objectives and keep the momentum going if you are willing to make adjustments to your routine.

Set Clear Goals:

It is really necessary to define your objectives in order to keep moving forward and continue on the route to achievement. When you have defined objectives, you will have a path to follow on your trip and will know exactly where you want to end up. This might help you maintain your motivation and keep your concentration, even if you run across difficulties or roadblocks along the way.

To ensure that your objectives are well defined, check that they are particular, quantifiable, attainable, relevant, and time-bound. Put your objectives in writing and make it a habit to look over them on a regular basis so that you can easily recall them. Create a strategy for attaining each of your objectives by breaking them down into a series of smaller, more doable steps.

Keeping tabs on how far you've come in the pursuit of your objectives is another crucial step. This might make it easier for you to maintain your motivation and make modifications as required. As you go along the path, be sure to celebrate your victories and see any obstacles that arise as a chance to learn and develop.

Celebrate Small Successes:

One of the most crucial strategies for keeping the momentum going and remaining on the road to success is to celebrate one's accomplishments, no matter how minor. Celebrate even the little victories, and you'll not only recognize your progress but also keep yourself encouraged to keep going ahead.

Find the checkpoints along the path to your objectives, and be sure to give yourself some recognition when you reach them so you can celebrate your progress. This might be doing something nice for yourself, such as going out to a nice dinner, giving yourself a day off to unwind, or just spending some time to think about how far you've come.

It is essential to keep in mind that success is not one achievement but rather the culmination of a number of incremental triumphs along the road. You may keep yourself motivated and dedicated to the route that leads to success by appreciating your little victories along the way.

Stay Accountable:

Keeping oneself responsible is a strong tactic that may help one keep moving forward and remain on the right road to achieve their goals. It is far more probable that you will follow through on your promises and continue progressing toward your objectives if you hold yourself, as well as others, responsible for your actions.

Consider working with an accountability partner or joining a support group in order to maintain your sense of responsibility. You may get criticism, feedback on your performance, and encouragement from this along the road. Tracking your progress toward your objectives and holding yourself responsible for continuing to work toward those objectives should also be high on your list of priorities.

Keep in mind that being accountable does not need you to be flawless; rather, it requires you to maintain your commitment to your objectives and make progress toward achieving them. You are able to keep moving forward and stay on the right track toward achievement if you remain responsible.

Encouragement and inspiration for continued personal development

Practice Self-Care:

For one's own continuing growth and development, self-care practices are absolutely necessary. Taking care of your physical, emotional, and mental health is very necessary if you want to keep your energy, attention, and motivation levels where they should be. Self-care may consist of a variety of pursuits, including physical activity, mental reflection, social interaction, and contact with the natural world.

Make taking care of yourself a top priority in your day-to-day activities if you want to make it a habit. Make sure you give yourself time every day to engage in activities that are beneficial to your body, mind, and spirit. In order to avoid exhaustion and burnout, make getting enough rest and relaxation a top priority and take breaks when they're called for.

The cultivation of self-compassion and the practice of treating oneself with love and understanding are also very essential. You may keep your energy levels, attention, and motivation up so that you can continue to work on your own personal growth if you engage in self-care practices.

Learn from Others:

The most effective method for one's ongoing personal growth is to acquire knowledge from the experiences of others. On your path, finding mentors, coaches, and role models to look up to may give you invaluable advice, motivation, and a sense of responsibility. You may also get knowledge from your friends and coworkers, who can provide you with fresh viewpoints and information.

Seek out possibilities for mentoring, coaching, and networking in order to get knowledge from other people. Participate in personal development-oriented activities, such as going to seminars and conferences, reading books and articles, and becoming active in online networks.

Additionally, it is essential to maintain an openness to receiving feedback and criticism, particularly constructive criticism. Being open to the comments of others will assist you in recognizing blind spots and areas in which you can make improvements. You may speed up your own development and attain higher levels of achievement by picking up new skills from other people.

Stay Flexible and Adaptable:

To sustain one's own personal growth, it is necessary to have a flexible and adaptive mindset. Because of the unpredictability of life, you should be prepared to make adjustments to your plans and objectives on occasion. You may continue to make progress toward your objectives even in the face of unforeseen setbacks if you maintain a flexible and adaptive mindset.

Develop a development attitude and a resilient character if you want to maintain your flexibility and adaptability. Embrace change because it presents a chance for personal development and advancement. Be flexible and prepared to make changes to your plans as necessary, and have an open mind to potential new experiences and possibilities.

Keeping things in perspective and having a healthy sense of equilibrium is also very essential. Make the aspects of your life that are most important to you a priority, and be ready to let go of the things in your life that aren't helping you or serving you anymore. You will be able to gracefully and easily handle the twists and turns of life if you maintain your flexibility and adaptability.

Celebrate Your Progress:

An essential component of ongoing personal growth is the practice of celebrating one's own progress. Recognizing and appreciating your successes might assist you in maintaining your motivation and dedication to achieving your objectives. In addition to this, it has the potential to provide you with a feeling of success and happiness.

To properly appreciate how far you've come, it's important to stop and think about the accomplishments and benchmarks along the way. Recognize the many hours of toil and commitment that it took to bring you to this point in your life. Share your victories with the people around you, and allow them to serve as motivation for you to keep pushing ahead.

Keep in mind that achieving your goals in terms of personal growth is a process, not an endpoint. You can keep moving forward toward your objectives and preserve your momentum if you celebrate the accomplishments you achieve along the road.

Conclusion

The path to success and riches is a multi-step process that calls for an in-depth comprehension of the ideas and routines that support both personal and monetary development. Throughout this book, we have discussed these fundamental factors and offered a road map that may serve as a guide for you on the way to achieving success and living a prosperous life.

The first thing that we did was investigate the routines of profitable and successful people. Specifically, we focused on how important it is to have self-control, perseverance, and a solid work ethic in order to establish a solid groundwork for future success. You may begin to build the attitude and behaviors that are indicative of individuals who have gained success and financial security by learning and adopting these habits. This will allow you to make progress toward achieving success and financial security.

This trip requires you to break free from the limits of the standard 9 to 5 mindset, which may impede creativity and limit your capacity to think beyond the boundaries of normal work arrangements. Breaking free from these constraints is an essential part of this journey. You may open up new doors to progress and personal satisfaction in your life if you are willing to question the established order and look into potential other routes.

In addition to this, we underlined the value of making even little adjustments while laying the groundwork for long-term success. Modifications to your routines and frame of mind, even if they are just a little, may have a significant impact on your life if you apply them regularly. You may gradually modify your life and build a strong foundation for future accomplishments if you put your attention on these very few adjustments.

The development of a mentality conducive to achievement is another essential component of this journey. Developing a constructive and proactive outlook on life, outlining your objectives, and retaining a firm faith in your capacity to accomplish those objectives are all necessary steps in this process. A mentality for success involves not just thinking positively but also acting consistently and learning from one's mistakes in order to keep moving ahead. Thinking positively is simply one component of this attitude.

The need to maintain a steady course was a recurring subject throughout the whole book. Your actions and choices, if they are consistent with one another, will generate momentum, which will carry you toward the results you want, as well as stimulate the creation of new habits and the accomplishment of objectives. You can tap into the transforming power of consistency if you cultivate it, which will also help you maintain long-term success.

Building your relationship base and your professional network are essential components of achieving success and growing your wealth. The ability to get access to priceless resources and opportunities may be gained through cultivating strong connections with persons who share similar values and by establishing these connections in the first place. You may improve your chances of being successful in both your personal and professional lives if you put effort into expanding your network and making the cultivation of relationships a top priority.

It is essential to both one's personal and one's financial development to make investments in oneself and one's future. This involves a wide variety of actions, including maintaining a healthy lifestyle, developing new skills, searching out educational opportunities, and creating a solid support system. You are establishing the basis for a rich and rewarding future by making the development of yourself and your personal relationships a top priority.

We also discussed a variety of methods for amassing money, with an emphasis placed on the significance of having a solid grasp of the fundamentals behind the creation of numerous income streams, as well as savings and investments. You may attain financial independence and the ability to follow your goals and desires without being constrained by money if you put these techniques into practice and let your wealth develop over time.

In conclusion, we agreed that the process of making changes that are long-lasting is a particular and unique adventure for each person. You will be able to alter your life and construct a path toward success and prosperity that is suited to your individual requirements and goals if you accept the concepts and techniques that are presented in this book and put them into practice. You will be well-equipped to overcome difficulties and build a future that is defined by your own vision of success if you are determined, consistent, and have a growth mindset. The path may be tough, but if you do so, you will be able to create a future that is defined by your own vision of success.

In conclusion, keep in mind that the quest for success and money is a journey, not a destination, that one takes during one's whole life. As you go forward along this route, it is very necessary to have a flexible and resilient mindset while also maintaining an openness to gaining knowledge from your experiences. You may release your full potential and build a future that represents your own vision of success and prosperity if you internalize the ideas and habits that are taught in this book and continuously apply them to your life. This book will help you do both of these things.

You should allow this book to act as a source of motivation for you, leading you toward a future that is better and more meaningful. As you begin out on your life-changing adventure, make it a point to welcome the challenge, recognize the significance of consistency, and cultivate a development attitude. The ideas and practices that are presented in this book are only the beginning; if you give yourself enough time, effort, and tenacity, you will continue to discover new insights and tactics that will further accelerate you toward your objectives.

As you make progress, maintain an attitude that is open to learning from other people, sharing the experiences you've had, and helping the people around you on their own roads to achievement. The path to long-term transformation involves not just one's own personal development but also the cultivation of a community of persons who share similar values and perspectives and who are able to encourage, motivate, and provide support to one another in their common quest for success and fulfillment.

In the end, the ultimate measure of success is not merely determined by the riches that one amasses or the plaudits that one receives; rather, it is defined by the person that one becomes along the course of their endeavours. Embrace the process, make consistent efforts toward development and progress, and be loyal to the ideals and goals you've set for yourself at all times.

As you get to the last page of this book, may it not mark the end of a chapter in your life but rather the beginning of a new one, one that is filled with the achievement of your goals and the establishment of a legacy that is a reflection of your best ideals. What you are capable of doing is only limited by your level of dedication, level of resolve, and level of perseverance.

Your route to long-term transformation, sustained success, and increased wealth may be navigated with the help of the ideas and practices that are explained in this book. And as you go on, keep in mind the wise words of novelist Napoleon Hill, who once remarked, "Whatever the mind can conceive and believe, it can achieve." In other words, whatever the mind can imagine and believe, it can do.

References

Covey, S. R. (1989). The 7 Habits of Highly Effective People. New York, NY: Free Press. Retrieved from https://archive.org/details/sevenhabitsofhi00cove_1

Ferriss, T. (2007). The 4-Hour Workweek: Escape 9-5, Live Anywhere, and Join the New Rich. New York, NY: Harmony Books. Retrieved from https://archive.org/details/4hourworkweek00ferr_0

Clear, J. (2018). Atomic Habits: An Easy & Proven Way to Build Good Habits & Break Bad Ones. New York, NY: Avery. Retrieved from https://www.jamesclear.com/atomic-habits

Dweck, C. S. (2006). Mindset: The New Psychology of Success. New York, NY: Ballantine Books. Retrieved from https://www.mindsetonline.com/

Gerber, J. (2020). The Power of Consistency: Prosperity Mindset Training for Sales and Business Professionals. Hoboken, NJ: Wiley. Retrieved from https://www.weldonlong.com/the-power-of-consistency/

Misner, I. R., & Donovan, B. (2016). Networking Like a Pro: Turning Contacts into Connections. Irvine, CA: Entrepreneur Press. Retrieved from https://www.entrepreneur.com/book/networkinglikea pro

Siebold, S. (2010). How Rich People Think. London, UK: London House Press. Retrieved from http://www.howrichpeoplethinkbook.com/

Kiyosaki, R. T. (1997). Rich Dad Poor Dad: What the Rich Teach Their Kids About Money That the Poor and Middle-Class Do Not! Scottsdale, AZ: Plata Publishing. Retrieved from https://www.richdad.com/

Bridges, W., & Bridges, S. (2016). Managing Transitions: Making the Most of Change. Philadelphia, PA: Da Capo Lifelong Books. Retrieved from https://www.williambridges.com/

Eker, T. H. (2005). Secrets of the Millionaire Mind: Mastering the Inner Game of Wealth. New York, NY: HarperCollins. Retrieved from https://www.harveker.com/

Robbins, T. (2014). Money: Master the Game – 7 Simple Steps to Financial Freedom. New York, NY: Simon &

Schuster. Retrieved from https://tonyrobbins.com/money-master-the-game/

Duckworth, A. (2016). Grit: The Power of Passion and Perseverance. New York, NY: Scribner. Retrieved from https://angeladuckworth.com/grit-book/

www.ingramcontent.com/pod-product-compliance
Lightning Source LLC
Chambersburg PA
CBHW070546220526
45467CB00003B/1097